REMEMBERING
LOUIS L'AMOUR

With best wishes —

Reese Hawkins

Memoir
by
Reese Hawkins
and his daughter
Meredith Hawkins Wallin

REMEMBERING LOUIS L'AMOUR

First Printing .... April 2001
Second Printing .... July 2001

The book is published on acid free paper.

All photos from Hawkins L'Amour collection.

Cover photograph by Margaret Hawkins. Louis L'Amour sitting on deadfall
with background of Colorado Blue Spruce. *(Chapter Four)*

Authors - Reese Hawkins and his daughter Meredith Hawkins Wallin
Publisher - McCleery & Sons Publishing

International Standard Book Number 0-9700624-7-8
Printed in the United States of America

To granddaughters

Taresa Lilja Hawkins
Tamarie Alana Hawkins
Jessica Hawkins Wallin

FORWARD

Becoming a friend of a famous author might sound like a beautiful but whimsical dream. But for Reese and Margaret Hawkins and their family, the dream came true.

Mr. Hawkins, a retired Jamestown pharmacist who originally came to North Dakota from South Carolina, recalls the first L'Amour book he read, one that Margaret gave him in 1970. He liked the book so well he could not put it down until he finished it.

On a trip to California in 1972 Hawkins decided to contact this famous fiction writer, a native of Jamestown, to see if there was any chance they might meet. L'Amour invited Hawkins to join him for lunch and that was the beginning of a great friendship.

In *Remembering Louis L'Amour* Hawkins and his coauthor, daughter Meredith Hawkins Wallin, focus on Louis L'Amour as a writer and as a person, referring especially to episodes from their family's friendship with L'Amour and the L'Amour family. The Hawkinses were guests a number of times in the L'Amour home in Los Angeles. Occasionally Reese Hawkins would accompany L'Amour on autographing sessions and speaking engagements. Primarily through these visits the authors take us to the sites of some of the stories and describe those places and how L'Amour wove them into his fiction. Reese Hawkins effectively assumes the role of a willing and curious student, asking questions and interpreting and reflecting on what the famous author said. Like Hawkins, L'Amour also comes across in *Remembering Louis L'Amour* as a willing and curious student. He approached his writing as a scholar. Discussions between Louis and Kathy L'Amour and the Hawkinses on such diverse topics as Navajo rugs and kachina figures and how pemmican was made, demonstrate how L'Amour's hungry and encyclopedic mind was always on the lookout for material that might appear later in his writings.

Through Hawkins and his daughter we learn something of L'Amour as a writer, for example, the fact that at any one time he might have the beginnings of twenty stories on file and occasionally would switch back and forth between two stories. More than writing habits, however, the reader experiences L'Amour's amazing sense of place. In his years of traveling the country from job to job he had come to know a wide range of Western figures, including Indians and pioneers and even some gunfighters and outlaws. In *Remembering Louis L'Amour* the reader sees L'Amour as one who listened to and learned from all kinds of people.

The Hawkinses dispel the notion that all westerns are little more than rough-and-tough, shoot'em-up action. In their discussion of L'Amour and the excerpts from his writings and speeches, they demonstrate his strong interest in history and the social forces that brought immigrants to America and the West and the dynamics that helped them survive and establish communities. While L'Amour is known as a writer who depicted a great deal of action, his sensitivity toward the plight of settlers, Indians, both the fortunate and the unfortunate, and even the social outcasts play an important role in his fiction. The high moral code and strong community values that infuse his writings and his speeches came not only from his family, as his widow Kathy suggests, but also from his youth in Jamestown.

In his speech at the dedication of the North Dakota Heritage Center in Bismarck, L'Amour stated that he wrote "for the people who do the work of the world, who live on the land or love the land, people who make and bake and struggle to make ends meet, for the people who invent, who design, who build, for the people who do." The fact that Louis L'Amour resonated with so many of these readers has been amply demonstrated by Reese Hawkins, who has done so much to help "The people who do" all over the world become acquainted with this famous fiction writer.

What Reese Hawkins and Meredith Hawkins Wallin have produced with this book about a friendship with an author is a great contribution to our knowledge of L'Amour as well as of literature of the American West.

Dr. James E. Coomber
Professor and Chair, Department of English
Concordia College - Moorhead, Minnesota
March 10, 2001

TABLE OF CONTENTS

A FRIENDLY WORD TO THE READER

My name is Reese Hawkins. Louis L'Amour (pronounced Louie) was my very good friend. So how, you may ask, did a friendship develop between a small-town pharmacist and a world-class writer who has sold more than three hundred million books? A small town, Jamestown, North Dakota, brought us together. It was Louis L'Amour's home town.

I grew up in South Carolina. Toward the end of World War II, our destroyer, U.S.S. Roe, returned to San Francisco after sixteen months duty in the Pacific. On arrival at Mare Island Naval Base July 29, 1945, overhaul of our ship began. This was still continuing when the war ended.

Margaret Benson of Bottineau, North Dakota and I met at the Officers Club on Mare Island Naval Base. She was a social worker for the Red Cross stationed at the amputee hospital. We were married on April 20, 1946 and decided to spend some of our lives in each home state.

In 1957 we bought an old-fashioned drug store on the main street in Jamestown. A town of 16,000, it is located along the James River in a valley which dips down out of flat prairie halfway between Bismarck and Fargo. It was a good town to raise children, and there our two, Meredith and Allan, grew up.

Three years ago, following two decades of retirement in South

Carolina, Margaret and I returned to Jamestown. We live on a crook of the James River, close to downtown and the library. We have been warmly welcomed home and are glad to be back in L'Amour country.

In the fall of 1975 I was wondering what to give Louis L'Amour for Christmas. This required some thought.

I left our drug store and walked along First Avenue toward the Alfred Dickey Public Library. Why not look through issues of *The Jamestown Sun* for several days through March 22, 1908, the day Louis was born? I did so and made notes on a number of items reported by the daily paper. From this research Margaret and I sent the following story to the L'Amours for Christmas:

The weather forecast reads: Fair tonight and Tuesday with continued mild temperature.

No. 1 hard wheat is selling for $1.06 a bushel. The new admission prices to the Bijou Theatre are 10 and 20 cents. Featured on tonight's program, in addition to other forms of entertainment, are several CAMERA GRAPHS — *The Bad Boy at the Wedding*, *Stolen Child's Career*, and *Holdup in Calabria*. For those who prefer not to walk home after dark, a 3 P.M. matinee is in the offering.

For those of us who aren't privileged to live where home cooked meals are served, the Capital Cafe offers special combination tickets — 21 meals for $ 5.00.

Last Saturday night, Miss Helen West and Mrs. Chase were hostesses for one of "the prettiest dancing parties" the city has seen in many a year. This was the opinion of the majority in attendance. It is reported one of the most novel of the figures was a *Firefly Waltz* in which the girls wore sticks of burning incense in their hair and danced in the darkened rooms.

Tonight there will be a crowd of people in the Opera House

applauding the Great McEwen, billed as an accomplished magician and world hypnotist.

The North Coast Limited arrived on schedule at 4:05 A.M.

The local public library has just received two recent additions of great value. The first was <u>English Men of Letters</u> by John Mosley, a set of 38 volumes purchased by the library. The second addition is two volumes of Bernard Shaw's plays, <u>Pleasant and Unpleasant</u>, given by Alfred Dickey.

Yesterday was Sunday, the twenty-second day of March. On that day an event took place in this town that was more important than the state of the weather, more exciting than an evening of dancing, and much more valuable than additions to the library. To a mother was born an infant son, Louis Dearborn L'Amour. Sometime in the future he will say, "It all began in Jamestown, so long ago."

I wonder what the Jamestown librarian thought of this newborn baby boy several years later. Large for his age, he was a very good-looking boy who spent time in the library almost every day after school. Many a day he read there until it closed.

CHAPTER 1

LOUIS L'AMOUR: LEADING THE PACK

For as long as he could remember, Louis L'Amour wanted to be a writer. His mother encouraged this, suggesting the children write letters to relatives and friends. Then, at thirteen, his serious reading began with The Genius of Solitude. Socrates became his hero.

According to an article in the June 10, 1998 issue of *The New York Times*, L'Amour had in print ninety novels, twenty-one collections of short stories, four works of non-fiction and one book of poetry. With more than three hundred million books in print by June of 1998, he had become one of the fastest-selling writers of all time.

One of his earliest memories was sitting on his grandfather's knee listening to him tell stories of those who settled in North Dakota and of the Indians who were native to the area. L'Amour often said, "If you take time to listen to the old people, you will learn from them." This was one of his prime sources for gathering background information used in his writing.

Louis began blazing his trail in 1923 when, at the age of fifteen, he and his family left Jamestown, North Dakota to settle in Oklahoma. Soon after this he struck out on his own, moving from job to job and library to library. In between those libraries, those oases of learning, he carried along a pocketful of the series of Little Blue Books published by Haldeman-Julius Publications of Gerard, Kansas. They sold for five to fifteen cents each.

He told me of riding a bus into Portland, Oregon on a rainy night. He had been promised a job that would be available in the next few days. All he had in his pocket was a small amount of change. When he got off the bus, after some inquiries, he was able to get a room in a very old run-down house. He took that room because it was cheap and it was near the library.

For two or three days he went to the library when it opened and read all day to keep his mind off his hunger. He often said, "I am as clearly a product of libraries as anyone could be."

He spent twenty years moving around the world, working at one job long enough to get enough money to move on. Seeing the country was of more interest than keeping a job.

His first job was skinning dead cattle in West Texas. Following that he was a hay shocker, longshoreman, elephant handler, lumberjack, sawmill hand, flume builder and fruit picker. In between these jobs he boxed professionally fifty-nine times, winning over fifty of the fights.

If you and I had walked in his shadow, we would have mined in the west, traversed India on foot, been shipwrecked in the West Indies, been an instructor in the Chinese army and been stranded on the Mojave Desert. During all these years this persevering, astute and observing Louis L'Amour was accumulating knowledge that would later flow from his fingertips to the pages of his books.

I don't know just when L'Amour wrote the following poem. It must have been during those years of wandering. This poem is among thirty-six he published in his first book, Smoke From This Altar, 1939 by Lusk Publishing Company, Oklahoma City, Oklahoma.

I wandered along the dusty way
  seeking the dawn of another day,
    like a drifting chip on a lonely stream
    like a breath of wind or a vagrant dream
  a forgotten soul on a weary quest
searching for home and love and rest.

I wandered along the dusty way
  and found my idols with feet of clay,
    my letters were ashes, my castles dust—
    the sword I wielded eaten by rust,
  my dreams were shattered — a heavy load
is all that is left on a winding road.

L'Amour did find his home, a beautiful house not far from UCLA in Los Angeles. He found his love, Kathy, his wife of thirty-two years.

CHAPTER 2

FLYING TO A HOMETOWN WELCOME

So what makes Louis L'Amour different from other writers? How did I come to read and admire his stories so much?

In the fall of 1970 Margaret brought a paperback to the prescription department of our store and asked me if I knew Louis L'Amour was a native of our town, Jamestown. I did not.

I set L'Amour's book aside, took it home with me that night and finished reading it before I went to sleep. Not since my early teens had I read westerns.

It was something unusual to keep me up that late. The first page involved me in the story. I became a silent partner following his leading character through the trees and down into the valley. Listening to the writer speak, I liked what I heard.

"This fellow L'Amour has something!" I told Margaret the next morning at breakfast. From that point on I began reading all of his novels as soon as the distributor delivered them to our store.[1]

Then in November of 1971 Margaret returned from a meeting of her book club, Portfolio, where the Alfred Dickey librarian had given a talk about four Jamestown authors. L'Amour and his sister Edna were among them. At the time Margaret served as a member of the Library Board. She immediately wrote L'Amour and his sister Edna to request photographs for the "Famous North

---

[1] Walz Pharmacy (formerly Hawkins Drug) on the main street in Jamestown, North Dakota still stocks a complete selection of L'Amour's books.

Dakotans" display in our drug store. Both answered by return mail.

The next week Margaret wrote Mrs. William Guy, the wife of North Dakota's governor, complimenting her on a recent television appearance. In the same letter she suggested Louis L'Amour be considered for the Theodore Roosevelt Rough Rider Award. This is the highest honor the State of North Dakota bestows on one of its native sons or daughters.

Governor Guy answered they did not know L'Amour was a native of North Dakota. His name was added to the list of more than thirty who had been nominated. We later learned both the Governor and his wife were L'Amour readers.

The following February of 1972, as I was shaving, I heard over the radio that Louis Dearborn L'Amour would receive the Theodore Roosevelt Rough Rider Award. It would be presented in Jamestown, where he and his sister Edna LaMoore Waldo[2] would receive Honorary Doctor's Degrees of Literature from Jamestown College. L'Amour would give the commencement address.

In the middle of March I made plans to travel to Margaret's sister's home in Pasadena, California to assist their mother on her return flight to North Dakota. Margaret suggested I write Mr. L'Amour to see if he might see me. Upon arrival at the David and Georgine Coleman residence in Pasadena, there was a message from L'Amour: "If you arrive before eleven o'clock call me, if not, get in touch with me in the morning."

I reached him before eleven and he invited me to join him for lunch in the Polo Lounge of the Beverly Hills Hotel. I found out later he often liked to get away from his writing to meet someone for a business lunch or just enjoy a social hour. He was well known at the Polo Lounge, in fact had his own table.

By then I had read some twenty of his novels. I had a perception, an insight, of what L'Amour was implanting in the minds of his readers. I asked many questions about his life and writing

---

[2] Edna kept the family's spelling of L'Amour. Edna LaMoore Waldo authored several books, best known is <u>Dakota</u>.

and listened to his answers with extreme interest. We talked for two hours.

He was personable and friendly. I told him what an honor it was to be chosen to receive the Theodore Roosevelt Rough Rider Award and encouraged him to bring Kathy, Beau and Angelique with him on his trip to North Dakota. The family had never been to North Dakota and Louis had not returned since he left when he was fifteen years old. He said he and Kathy had been thinking of this but their children would miss some school.

The whole family came. At the Jamestown Airport they were greeted by a Jamestown College band, an authentic chuck wagon and several individuals on horseback who looked as if they had just ridden out of one of Remington's paintings.

For three days Margaret and I entertained the children while Louis and Kathy made the rounds of special activities. We took Beau and Angelique to the places their grandparents had frequented. We showed them the house where they lived and the city hall where their grandfather[3] was an alderman.

We showed them where their father went to school and the Alfred Dickey Library where he read. Just as we had with our own two children, we took them canoeing on the James River, and watched them run through an adjacent field of almost waist-high prairie grass. Between these visits we stopped at our house for cool drinks and Margaret's Buffalo Cookies[4].

When he returned home Louis wrote,

"Our visit to Jamestown was without a doubt one of the crowning experiences one could have, and from first to last, it was a happy occasion."

This was the beginning of our friendship with the Louis L'Amour Family. Margaret and I were a link to Louis' hometown, to where his journey began. In the years that followed they lovingly treated us like family.

---

[3] Dr. L.C. LaMoore, a veterinarian, was civic-minded and a good story-teller.
[4] Recipe at end of chapter.

Margaret and I spent a week with the L'Amours in Colorado, taking daily excursions out of Durango. Our daughter Meredith joined us during another week with them when we visited the Kings Mountain National Battlefield in South Carolina and continued up through the Blue Ridge Mountains to Washington, DC. Later Margaret and I spent several days with Louis in Tennessee.

Many times we were guests in the L'Amour home. I accompanied Louis on autographing sessions, and when he spoke to booksellers, members of a chamber of commerce and to Indian students. His sharing enriched my life.

In 1981, Dr. L'Amour received two additional Honorary degrees, a Doctor of Letters from North Dakota State University and a Doctor of Literature from the University of LaVerne. Later, he received an honorary degree of Law from Pepperdine University.

On rare occasions the Congress of the United States awards a Congressional Gold Medal to recognize and honor individuals who have contributed to the history of our country. George Washington received the first.

On September 24, 1983 President Reagan presented Louis L'Amour with the 81st Congressional Gold Medal at a White House ceremony. L'Amour was the first novelist to receive this award. Later President Reagan honored him with the Presidential Freedom Award.

Do not make in hot, humid weather.

1962 PILLSBURY STATE AWARD WINNER

(Sketch by J. A. Kirkpatrick,
Jamestown's Western Artist)

Hawkins Buffalo Cookies

1 cup butter	⅛ teaspoon salt
1 cup brown sugar	2 teaspoons soda
¼ cup molasses	1 teaspoon ginger
1 egg	1 teaspoon cloves
2 cups flour	1 teaspoon cinnamon

Cream butter and sugar well, beat in egg, add molasses and ingredients which have been sifted together. Chill a few hours. Roll, cut with BUFFALO COOKIE CUTTER. Bake 8 min. at 375 degrees. Makes 50 crisp cookies.

Frost part of head and body with a layer of frosting and dip into a bowl of chocolate cake decorations.

Frosting: Melt 1 sq. chocolate, 1 tablespoon butter. Add 3 tablespoons cream and one cup sifted confectioners sugar.

JAMESTOWN, NORTH DAKOTA
"Home Of The World's Largest Buffalo"

CHAPTER 3

ENTERING L'AMOUR COUNTRY: THE HOME OF THE SACKETTS

"Look at the train! Look at the train!" exclaimed an excited Angelique L'Amour, age nine. It was August of 1973. Margaret and I were spending some time with the L'Amour family in Durango, Colorado.

The engineer seemed to hear her. He responded by engaging the whistle for a long time. We watched the heavy, coal-fired steam locomotive pull out of the station with determined "chug chugs" as it began its upward pull to Silverton. The Durango and Silverton narrow gauge train departed Durango from 479 Main Avenue. The train made its maiden trip in 1882 and had been in continuous use ever since.

"There are two of them," Angelique said. "One leaves at 8:40 and the other at 9:00. We will all go on it Friday."

Margaret wondered how many people could be seated on the train at a time. "About four hundred or so, depending on the makeup of coaches," Louis answered.

As the speed of the train increased, the "chugs" became more frequent until they blended into a continuous sound. With one last whistle the train disappeared around a curve and we started our car trip into the San Juan Mountains.

The L'Amours spent time during the summer in Durango and this year we were their guests for a week. Their enthusiasm was contagious. For Margaret and me it was better than being in the audience at a hit show on Broadway. Here we were on stage with members of the cast.

Born as a mining and smelting center midst the gold and silver rushes, Durango's downtown reflected the lively spirit of those early days. After our week's stay at the Strater Hotel and daily trips to some of the most scenic sections of Colorado, we had absorbed some of the flavor of the old west. It was a firsthand study, a live history lesson. Our teachers were Louis L'Amour and Louis' good friend, Don Demarest.

This day was to be a memorable adventure for Margaret and me. Newcomers to the San Juan mountains, we were to be introduced to their greatness and majesty by L'Amour and Demarest who knew the area so well. Geologically speaking this was the youngest range of mountains in Colorado. For this reason they presented a more jagged, precipitous appearance.

With Kathy driving, we settled into the station wagon and were on our way. I had looked at the map before we left. We were traveling on Highway 160 west from Durango. Mancos was twenty-seven miles from Durango and Cortez was forty-three. We planned to go there tomorrow.

Angelique called out, "Mom, on the way up we will have to stop and see my horses."

"After we go up to the Cumberland," Kathy said. "We will see them on the way back."

"This is the Animas River," Louis pointed out, "the river of lost gold."

"Where does it originate, Louis?" I asked.

"Up high in the San Juan Mountains. Then it flows down into the San Juan River and eventually into the Colorado River."

As the miles slowly slipped past, the L'Amours described some of the country. We saw a couple of bicyclists. Angelique said one time they had rented tandem bicycles.

"Who did that?" I asked.

"My mama, daddy, me and Beau. I rode with my daddy and my mama and Beau rode together."

"Would you rather ride with your mama or your dad on a tandem?" I asked.

"My dad." Angelique laughed.

"Why?"

"Because mama hadn't ridden in a long time. My dad is used to walking."

"This is beautiful country," Margaret commented.

"Those are the twin peaks," Louis said. "They are quite a landmark around here. You can see them from way up the mountain where we are going. Up here a little ways is a small creek. We are kind of interested in a piece of property that lies up ahead of it."

"Is it erosion that makes the top of the peaks stick out?" I asked.

"That's the reason, the erosion. Mostly wind, some from water a long long time ago. Most of the debris down at the bottom has fallen off the peaks."

"There will be no tops on the peaks if this process continues."

"Eventually," Louis said. "But it will be a long, long time. A lot of this country is broken off from those high tablelands, mesas they call them, you know. There's the creek I mentioned. I am very interested in a ranch up at the end of it.

"Gold mines are all through this country, but oddly enough most of the really rich values, the rich gold and silver, were found way at the top of the mountains above the timber line. They can work them for only a short season because of the heavy snow in the winter.

"Up there where we are going is a gold mine. I went down in it a couple of years ago and got a piece of gold for Kathy. It was a very old mine."

Beau, age twelve, called our attention to a mine shaft along the road.

Louis told us old prospectors' holes and shafts just like that one were all along the hills. "There is a lot of coal in this country," he said.

"Both of these we will see in a moment are coal mines," Beau told us. "This one here is partially burnt."

"Burned on the surface a long time?" I asked.

"Yeah."

"How deep do they go to reach coal?" I inquired, sighting a shaft opening into the mountain.

"Most of the coal is on the surface," Louis said. "The Shalako Incorporated Company owns several thousand acres of coal out here. We have a deal pending now to sell the mining rights to a big company for a lot of money."

Beau told of one mine from which fifty million dollars worth of gold was taken. Louis verified this figure.

"You mentioned the million dollar highway yesterday," I said. "Is it on this route we are taking today?"

"No, it's between Silverton and Ouray. Ouray is named for old Chief Ouray who was a chief of the Utes. He and his wife were two famous Indians in this part of the country and always friends of the white man. Ouray was a very very bright man, very competent leader."

"How do Indians get names like that?" Beau asked.

"Indian names came from a variety of things. Some of them were named for animals, a particular animal or spirit animal. Sometimes they were named from something they saw during their initiation ceremony or some experience they had. Sometimes an Indian would have two or three names in his lifetime. Among some tribes of Indians the name is never told to anyone for fear it will give power to the person who has the name."

"What would they call them?" Beau asked.

"They would call them by some other name but this is their real name."

"They had a secret name then?" I asked.

"The secret name," Louis answered, "is their real name. But almost no one knows it except perhaps their mother and father."

"Do they sometimes get rid of one name and take another?" I asked. "Is this the individual who does that?"

"Yes, sometimes. Sometimes the tribe does it. An Indian performs some great feat of valor and he may be named for that. Or he may be named for some characteristic that he has, like one of the famous Sioux Chiefs whose name was Man Afraid of His Horses. He wasn't afraid of his horses, he was afraid people would steal his horses."

"Oh!" Margaret said. "He probably had nightmares about someone stealing his horses."

"It could be," Louis responded.

"I don't know the exact origin of Sitting Bull's name," he continued. "It is very likely he got it when he reached the age of puberty. An Indian would go out in the hills alone and he would go through some initiation rites. He would dream and sometimes he would take the name of the animal he saw in his dream. And very likely he saw a sitting buffalo, because his name really was Sitting Buffalo, not Sitting Bull."

"We will probably be climbing for a long time," I said, looking ahead at the high mountains.

"Yes," said L'Amour. That tower over there is the only man-made object within sight of our town. We will plant some trees to screen it."

"We are still west of Durango, aren't we?" asked Margaret.

"Yes," Louis answered. "See those little clouds over there on the horizon? We are going to be high up in those mountains in a very few minutes."

"The ones with a little snow on top?" I asked.

"Much more snow than it looks like."

"What elevation will Shalako[1] be?"

"Just over 8000 feet," Louis said.

"Look, look!" Margaret suddenly said.

On the edge of Hesperus was a billboard proclaiming,

```
ENTERING  LOUIS L'AMOUR COUNTRY
          S H A L A K O
        HOME OF THE SACKETTS
```

"Now the land that belongs to Shalako Inc. begins right along in here," Louis told us. "We own a piece back there of about two hundred acres, then we own right along the highway, all this land. I am talking about the Corporation now, not me personally. And on down just before the road curves, this piece right in here we own."

"The town of Shalako will be off the road a ways?" I asked.

"Yes, right here on this bench is where the motel is going to be. There will be a motel and restaurant there and a coffee shop just over this stretch down below and a filling station down there."

Louis pointed out the exact location of the coffee shop and another filling station as we passed. "The company now owns that store and the post office."

We pulled off the road to a motel where we met Don Demarest. He'd brought a thermos of coffee and a container of food. We transferred our things into Don's four wheel drive ve-

---

[1] Shalako was to be a composite replica of a small western town that existed during the period L'Amour wrote about.

hicle and climbed in after them, knowing we were in good hands with him at the wheel.

"The last scenes of my book <u>Treasure Mountain</u>," L'Amour explained, "took place up here in the Cumberland Basin where we are going. And Don, of course, knows all that country. He's been over it and, as he says, he just visualizes it when reading my book. He can see every bit of it. He knows the trail that I had my man, Tell Sackett, use to come up from the other side.

"Pretty quick I will show you the place where he came over the divide and down. Now the trail leads up to one of the old mines. In those days the big notch wasn't up there in the hills. They cut that through later. But there was a horse trail over there, a foot path at least, and you could come over the mountain up there."

"Well, this is it!" I happily exclaimed. "We're going to another place you wrote about."

COLORADO

Lizard Head Pass
10,222'

Silverton

McPhee
Reservoir

RICO

HIGHWAY 145

Cascade
Village

San Juan Scenic Byway

Electra
Lake

Stoner

Purgatory
Ski Area

Dolores River

Tamaron
Hilton

Hermosa Creek

Animas River

Dolores HIGHWAY
184

Lemon
Dam

Mancos

HIGHWAY 160

Hermosa
Trimble
Lane

CTY RD 240

Hesperus
Ski Area

Hot
Springs

Mesa Verde
National Park

Hesperus

Durango

Animas
Air Park

HIGHWAY
172

Mancos River

La Plata River

HIGHWAY 140

La Plata
County
Airport

Southern Ute
Indian Reservation

CHAPTER 4

TRACKING TREASURE MOUNTAIN IN COLORADO

"This is just like what we have growing in our yard in North Dakota," said Margaret, pointing out what she knew as larkspur. "Here it's growing wild."

"You called this something else.   What was it, Louis?" I asked.

"Lupine,"[1] he said. "The yellow flowers with the brown center look something like brown-eyed susan."

"They are all over Colorado," Margaret commented. "Is that the state flower?"

"No," Louis answered. "The Columbine. You will see that pretty quick. Some of the most beautiful flowers you have ever laid your eyes on."

Momentarily they came into view. A vast field, nature's yellow blanket spread out before us.

"Look at that!" exclaimed Margaret.

"Beautiful!" I added.

"Isn't it gorgeous?" L'Amour asked.

Looking ahead as we continued upward we saw large ragged

---

[1] It is any of a group of plants, genus lupinus of the pea family, bearing spikes of white, yellow, blue or purple flowers. [Latin lupinum, from lupus wolf; referring to the belief that the plant exhausts the soil.]

gaps in the forest framed by dark green trees. Through these open doors was clear crystal blue sky.

"I believe we are getting up to the timber line," I said.

"Yes," Louis said. "You have to get off the highway to experience beauty like this."

"We will see a lot of sheep up here," said Angelique.

Soon, as we saw the first snow which was in stark contrast to the field of flowers left behind, Angelique inquired about the snow in North Dakota, asking if there was any now. I told her I had once played golf in December, but that was quite unusual. Most of the time snow might begin falling in November and, in some cases, it did not melt until spring. Only during blizzards were some of the roads closed to traffic and this rarely happened. Margaret and Louis could have told Angelique all this because they both were born, and grew up in, North Dakota.

"The snow you see now is above the timber line," Louis said. "There are acres of snow up there in places. Much more than it looks like from here."

At this point the trail narrowed. I was concerned. "Suppose we meet another vehicle."

"With a wide load on it," Margaret added.

"Nothing we can do," I said, stating the obvious. "Someone has to back up. I am looking down a vertical drop of . . ."

"Probably five hundred feet," L'Amour said. "There are places up here you have to look twice to see the bottom. First look as far as you can. Then look again the rest of the way."

Louis kidded us often, especially when the children were with us. Don Demarest was silent, concentrating on driving.

Above the tree line there were some level grassy areas. We passed and greeted a motorcyclist standing beside his bike next to the road. A profusion of Columbine in its natural habitat left us speechless for a moment.

Louis asked Don if he had ever explored one of the high mountains we could see in the distance.

"No I haven't," Don answered.

"Some of the peaks must rise to 14,000 feet," L'Amour continued. "This is a cirque,[2] an area created by a glacier."

Then Louis indicated a notch ahead. "Now Tell Sackett was riding down that trail when it was only a horse trail. He was shot at and he rolled off his horse."[3]

An area of red flowers came into view. Louis said sometimes they have different shades depending on the mineral content of the soil.

"Angelique is trying to tell you about that old mine over there," Don said, pointing it out.

"I have worked on a lot of movies. We did one up there called *Lock Stock and Barrel*, an NBC world wide premiere. It was the first one I ever got a producer to do up here in this country. We used a four-wheel drive. In July of 1970 we had up here Burgess Meredith, Tim Mathison, Belinda Montgomery, Claude Akins and Jack Albertson, one of the old-timers."

"Was that a western?" asked Margaret.

"Yes'm. We did it up here. We needed a mine in this location because we wanted to use these boilers which were back in the old Cumberland mine. So we went over to the hillside and we just dug in there a little ways. Hung some black plastic in there and our cameras were set up right where we are now.

"Burgess Meredith and others came on horseback. Tim and Belinda came in a wagon train right over the top of it. And the humorous part about it is, one of the old local prospectors up here who had gone up earlier in the year, way back in the Hermosa area and spent the summer over there, was coming back down in the fall. He came down the road and looked over there and saw that mine entrance. It really threw him because there had never been a

---

[2] Cirque is a circular space, especially a bowl-like depression having steep walls.
[3] Treasure Mountain, chapter 21.

mine there. While he was gone during the summer one got built!"

"Don," Margaret asked, "how did you get the movie companies to come here?"

"Well, I act as a location scout for the studios."

"Oh, I see!"

"We have done about eighteen major pictures here. Did you see *Butch Cassidy and the Sundance Kid* with Paul Newman? I did that with them in 1968."

"Do you also take a part in them?"

"The only one I have been in was one of Louis', *How the West was Won.* That was before I knew Louis, which was quite an odd coincidence. Back in the '50's I did that and twenty-some years later I know Louis."

"Wasn't that on television just last winter?" Margaret asked.

"Oh yeah, they replay it quite often."

Kathy said the first time she saw it was on a wide screen.

We saw a couple more motorcyclists coming down. Camping equipment was strapped on their motorcycles and packs on their backs.

Margaret asked, "You must have corresponded a lot with those studios, didn't you?"

"Well, no. Not so much paperwork, just physical. We get copies of the script and we have to find a waterfall or something that will meet their needs. We are going to do another one next spring, a major picture."

"Do you know the name of it?"

"I don't know the name of it. Universal Studios will do it, I think."

"This is the kind of area many people who visit Colorado miss entirely," L'Amour said.

"That's right," agreed Margaret. "And many of the people who live here too. Like New York. Some of the people who have lived there all their lives have never been to the Statue of Liberty."

Louis talked about hiking across to Taylor Lake, how long it would take and the high altitude which would get your wind. He said he hadn't done enough hiking around at this altitude to get acclimated to it. "But I walk a little more each time."

I asked Don if he gets used to the lack of oxygen.

"Oh yeah, the body adjusts to it," he said. "Takes quite a while to get fully adjusted to it."

Louis spoke up, "I want you to notice these beautiful fleecy white clouds and the blue sky. Don and I arranged that for you."

Margaret and I applauded.

From sea level the clouds would have been about 10,000 feet, but it seemed we could reach up and grab them. Looking across the vast Cumberland Basin, Louis pointed out peaks 14,000 feet high.

Suddenly we stopped. Louis, Don, and Kathy discussed a post in the center of the road blocking our passage. Kathy was concerned about getting our food to the location up ahead.

Two or three distant places were talked about but Kathy suggested, "This is so pretty right ahead. I think we should set up there."

"OK, we will stay here," Louis agreed.

"Whatever you want to do, Louis," Kathy said. "It's so nice to be over there in the woods instead of driving in the car all the time. Don't you want to take Reese and show him that hideout?"

"Yeah. I can carry this stuff down if you want to park here, Don."

"You going to hang something on the post?" Kathy asked Don after he got out of the Surburban.

"Going to take it out of the ground," Don replied.

Kathy asked why they put the post there.

"Well, they want to establish the road down there," Don said, "but I don't agree with them."

"You mean the federal government?" she asked.

"Yeah."

"What do we do if they find you moved it?" Louis asked Don.

"I don't know, I'll take care of it.."

Everyone was quiet while Don finished removing the post. Then he turned it over, put it down flat so the "NO VEHICLES ALLOWED" faced the ground.

"We can put the sign up when we go back," L'Amour said, as we drove right up to the campsite.

We stretched a bit while Don organized the unloading of the food and then started a fire.

The height of Pikes Peak came up in our discussion. Louis said one of his ancestors, Henry Dearborn, was in overall command of the American troops when they invaded Canada during the War of 1812. Brigadier General Zebulon Pike was under General Dearborn's command. It was from him Pike's Peak got it's name.

My interest led me to two sources: A book entitled, <u>The War of 1812</u>, and the <u>Encyclopædia Britannica</u>. This happened often. When Louis wrote about something or mentioned it in conversation, I wanted to know more about it.

Dearborn was born in southeastern New Hampshire. He left his medical practice and began his military career as a captain at the battle of Bunker Hill. He continued to serve, participating in the battles of Saratoga, Valley Forge and the siege of Yorktown.

He was a writer as were so many in L'Amour's family. The journal he kept during the war, including detailed accounts of the main engagements, became a valuable first-hand record of the major campaigns of the Revolutionary War.

Louis said General Dearborn was given command of the

Canadian campaign. Because of his advanced age, he did not want to assume the command at all.

The American troops, under the immediate command of Brigadier-General Zebulon Pike, who was under General Dearborn, led the attack against the British fort at York (now Toronto, Canada). They broke into the fortress.

In its retreat the British garrison set fire to the main magazine. Just as his victorious soldiers were breaking in, Pike was killed by the ensuing explosion when a rock fell on him. Nearly forty were killed and two hundred wounded.

"Last year we stood in that spot," L'Amour said, "where this battle took place."

"That was in Toronto in Canada?" Margaret asked. "And he was the one Pike's Peak was named after?"

"Yes," Louis said. "Actually he explored a lot out here, but he was responsible for holding back the development of the country quite a bit. He wasn't impressed by the great plains at all. When he began crossing them it was very dry and he called them the great American desert.

"For a long time people stopped moving because they thought there was a great big desert out there. And all that beautiful plains country in Oklahoma, Kansas, Texas, Nebraska, where they now grow such great wheat and corn crops, Pike thought was all desert.

"Another thing that held back the development of the country was the change. You see," Louis continued as he shifted position on the deadfall tree where he was sitting, "when the first people came over here from Europe, they settled in the eastern states where there was lots of timber. Then they came on west to Pennsylvania and Ohio where there was really dense timber. You couldn't see the sky. The cover was thick. It was all black under those trees . . . and they were great big trees. So whenever they wanted to build they felled the trees, cleared a space and used the logs to build a cabin.

"Then all of a sudden they came to the plains. They didn't know how to operate because they had always operated where there was lots of timber. They were stopped for quite a while by those plains. Then finally people began moving out across to go to California, and they learned how to build sod houses, you know. Then the soddy[4] came into being like we had in North Dakota in the early days. They didn't have the logs for a log cabin, so they built the soddies. Later, of course, they imported timber."

As Margaret and I listened to Louis tell about the delay of the movement of the frontier westward, we thought about the difference in the Great Plains during that time and the Midwest now. After the soddy came along, the forbidding and foreboding plains slowly became what they are today, vast fertile crop lands dotted with towns and a few large cities.

---

[4] Soddy was a cabin built from blocks of sod taken from the prairie.

CHAPTER 5

FOLLOWING TELL SACKETT'S FOOTSTEPS

"We are standing in the area now within ten feet of where Tell Sackett almost walked over the rim," L'Amour said. "He was leading his horse on a pitch black night with a woman's body over the saddle.[1] He almost stepped over the edge and this is a drop of about 1200 feet clear to the bottom. He wouldn't fall 1200 feet. He would fall about eight hundred feet and then probably roll about four hundred feet.

"We are looking over the great inner Cumberland basin from the top of the mountain near Cumberland pass," he continued. "It is a vast unpopulated area; there are no people in it. There have been some logging and mining claims down there. You can look across the country and see the needles off there in the distance. Most of those peaks over there on the skyline are above 14,000 feet.

"Back over in there is where Sackett took place, another one of my stories. If I remember correctly," L'Amour continued, indicating another direction, "this bald peak in here is, I believe, Engineering Mountain. When we get further over you will be able to see the Lizard, a great pointed peak that looks like a great lizard head sticking up. It towers about four hundred feet above the surrounding country and is a very noted landmark. There is Lizard

---

[1] The woman was unconscious, not dead. Treasure Mountain, chapter 22.

Head Pass that extends all the way to Ridgway. We will probably see that later on."

"We are going to have a picnic on this spot?" I asked.

"Right on this spot down here under the trees," L'Amour answered. "Right off to the left is the hideout where in Treasure Mountain the last fight was fought. I'll put my camera down now and help them. I think we will need another film pretty quick."

Louis and Beau had been taking moving pictures, switching the camera back and forth. Movies of places Louis was research-ing were frequently taken.

Kathy called out to Louis, "Get hold of Margaret, honey. Get hold of someone as you go down there Margaret. It's uneven you know."

Margaret had broken her ankle two months before this so-journ into the mountains. Kathy and Louis were both concerned. Margaret decided to stay with Kathy.

Don started a campfire in the shade of the Colorado Blue Spruce.

"I believe Louis is going to show me a cave in a minute," I said.

"No, not a cave, " he said.

Beau beat us to the doughnuts and said something with one in his mouth. I couldn't understand but didn't ask him to repeat it. Choking hazard, you know – the high altitude, shortness of breath, eating and talking at the same time.

All except efficient Kathy were gathered in a group. She was preparing the food for our cookout. The high elevation caused some shortage of breath, but in no way did it hamper our appetites.

"Reese," Louis said. "Walk over here and I'll show you the area where that fight took place.[2] Look right through here, you'll see some green grass and trees. In a minute I will show you some-thing you don't really expect to see."

---

[2] Treasure Mountain, chapter 24.

There was a little opening with a big tree lying across it. We moved toward the area followed by Beau, Angelique and Don.

"See, there is a little bench down there you would not even know existed until you are right on top of it."

"Isn't that something!"

"This is where Tell's father had his camp and where his father died. This is where the final fight took place between Tell and his enemy."

Beau added it was down there where Tell's father hid an old book.

"Yes," Louis said. "His father hid an old book. In fact it was right around that point of rock there."

"An old what?" Angelique asked.

"An old book. He made some notes in it. See this is a little bench down here. You could be back where the fire is and you wouldn't know this is here."

"And you call it a bench because it is a level area along the side of the mountain? " I asked.

"Yeah, that's right."

"There is something or other way over there," Beau said. "My dad thinks it is a fort, I think it's – I don't know."

"Well, what I think it is," Louis elaborated, "I think it was once a trapper's fort that was remade into a sheep pen. It may have been a sheep pen all the time – although I am kinda doubtful if a sheep herder would put as much work as in that.

"See that point right across the canyon over there? You can see a white spot there, some downed timber that's built into kind of a wall. I don't know if a sheep herder would have built in that particular place. He may have done it, but I think it was a trapper's fort that was abandoned and a sheep herder found some of the logs there and just added more logs, built it up and used it. I am going to go over there and dig one of these days, work it over with a metal detector first, then do a little digging just for fun."

"Gold will show up on a metal detector, won't it?" I asked.

"Yes, it will."

"What are you going to dig for?"

"Oh, I'm just looking for any relics I might find to identify the people who might have been there.

"Now right here ahead of us is a stairway I had put in here a couple thousand years ago so I could have it all set for you to go down to this bench."

"Let's see you go down it, go down it!" Angelique shrieked.

"You really think it is that old?" I asked.

"Yes, I think it is older than that probably," Louis answered.

"It was built by someone, wasn't it?"

"No, it's natural."

"How can you tell whether it's natural?" I asked Don. "The way the rocks extend out and everything?"

"The way the tree roots have grown around. They haven't been disturbed."

We started the climb down, Beau filming our descent until we reached the bench.

"This is the hideout," Louis explained. "From up above you can't even see this place. Actually you could put a company of soldiers down here. And nobody would have any idea they were here unless they came right up to the edge."

Not caring to approach too close to a vertical drop-off I asked, "From above, would I have to walk up to within a few feet of the edge before I could see this bench?"

"That's right."

"Then I don't think I would ever see it."

Don had brought along a copy of Treasure Mountain. Louis wrote something in it while we were standing there, right where the climax of the book took place – where Tell's father had his camp and where he died.

Looking out we saw white puffy clouds scattered across the transparent sky. The others started back up the old steps toward the campsite.

"Let's walk down over here," Louis said to me. "Of course, you have to realize there have been some changes going on in this country all the time and this story I wrote took place roughly one hundred years ago. This was pretty much then as it is now. Some of the trees are taller, some trees hadn't even sprouted here yet, some of those logs that are down over there now were live trees at that time, so you have to allow for a few changes that took place.

"I have army reports on much of this country. The army came in here and explored. Now here is a downed tree that's probably one hundred years old. That undoubtedly was growing and tall when the events in my story took place. I have read the army reports of this area about things that happened here."

"Knowing the age of the trees, Louis, you could just put them back up and describe the scene."

"Yes, that's practically what I did. There were some heavy falls of trees over here. Some of those have gone since I first came here. Right across this gap there were some large logs lying over there. That area a hundred years ago was almost impassable.

"You had to skirt around it. You could get by on foot, you know, very difficult to get by on a horse. This area right in here is what I'm speaking about.

"I ask questions," Louis continued, "of the men who have been around here for years. Now I skirted a lot of this country last year on the opposite side of these mountains with an old cowboy who had punched cows up here for sixty-odd years.

"Every time we passed a cutting where foresters, lumberjacks or anyone had cut down trees or somebody had felled trees for a log cabin, I'd ask him the age of the tree because he had been here when they were felled, you see. So from the condition of those trees I could get a pretty good idea of how long the trees had been on the ground.

"And I have been asking people these questions for years so I would have this knowledge and be able to pass it on. Let's walk over here a little ways."

As I listened to Louis, I recalled something he had told me earlier. Dean Dick Johns of the geology department, Stanford University, included in his introductory remarks to beginning classes, "If you really want to know what geology is all about, read the first chapter of Louis L'Amour's The Empty Land."

Louis paused every once in a while, mostly to accommodate me. We were at about 11,000 feet and my experience walking at this elevation was, to say the least, limited. Fact was, the only other place where I'd experienced elevations around 11,000 feet was in an airplane.

Angelique joined us again and we both listened to her dad.

"Here is a great tree which was standing a few years ago," said Louis, reaching up. "And right up here is a crack in the rock where Tell Sackett found his father's diary."

Is Treasure Mountain a true story?" Angelique asked.

"It's a fictional story, but it was laid in true surroundings and the actual situation was all true. The reason it is a treasure mountain is there really was a huge treasure buried here which is still not found."

"WHERE?" asked Angelique.

"It's over at Wolf Creek Pass. Remember the time we saw the whisky jack, that bird that came down out of the trees and picked popcorn from us? Remember that bird? Well, that was a whiskey jack. They are very friendly. They will take bread or anything you have to eat from you. And Wolf Creek Pass was right around the edge of Treasure Mountain."

"Dad, I want to go and try to find that treasure."

"Well, you might do that some time. It's very difficult to do. A lot of people have tried but nobody has found it.

"These men were sent out here by the French government to try and get gold because everybody in France was demanding that their colonies bring some gold to France like the Spanish colonies had done for Spain. So they sent this expedition out here to look for gold and they found gold.

"The Ute Indians attacked and got away with the gold. A few individuals got away with a little bit. Some of the individual stashes of gold have been found since, but the main stash, supposed to be worth thirty million dollars, has never been found. There were three hundred soldiers mining that gold."

We had made our way back to the campfire.

"A bald eagle just took off from this point," Don said, "and went clear down to the bottom. Something disturbed it."

I asked him to tell me his thoughts about this vast inner basin surrounded by a circle of very high mountains.

"It's so big you can't describe it. Well, I have taken so many people up here over the years from Georgia, Alabama and some other places. We get up here where you are looking off hundreds and hundreds of feet below. They just stand here with their tongues hanging out. They just don't believe that there is country like this. If they stay on a major highway in Colorado they miss seeing it."

"You can just sit here and look," I said, "for an hour or two, or even half a day."

Don said he had made over five hundred trips up here and hadn't seen it all yet.

"Are you hungry?" Angelique asked me.

"I think the idea we are getting," Louis said, "is that Angelique is hungry. One day Don saw twenty-six elk walking along that slope down by those trees."

"Sound really carries, doesn't it?" I asked Louis.

"What one should really do to understand this kind of country is not sit together but walk off alone about a quarter of a mile over there and just sit down and listen."

When we arrived back at the campfire, Don told us the story of how he met Louis.

"Bob was on his way in from California. Somewhere along the edge of Arizona he called me on the phone said he needed tickets for that night at the Melodrama.[3]

"Well, that thing is always sold out. I mean in the summertime there's just no way of getting tickets for it. So I said, 'What do you know, it is already sold out.'"

" 'I know it,' he said, 'but I still need the tickets. See what you can do.' So I called up Earle Barker, who owns the Strater Hotel. Of course Earle was a good friend of mine and still is. I told him I just had to have two tickets that night. He said, 'Well, you make it rough on a guy.'

"I said, 'I can't help that. I've still got to have two tickets'. Same deal as Bob had said.

"He said, 'All right, I'll see what I can juggle around and I will call you back in half an hour or so and let you know.'

"So he called me back and said, 'All right, the tickets are there in your name. Have them picked up when your party gets in.'

"When they arrived there that night," Don continued, "extra chairs had been placed at one of the tables at the melodrama and who is sitting there at the table but Kathy and Louis."

There was a chuckle in his voice as he said, "Of course those little tables are only about eighteen inches in diameter, you *got to get to know* the people sitting there.

"So anyhow they introduced themselves to each other. Louis told Bob what he was out here for. He was looking for a ghost town that he could build into a western village or something like

---

[3] This was a nightly production in the summer at the Strater Hotel in Durango. We attended one night with the L'Amours.

that.

"Bob said, 'Well, we've got a lot of land up the canyon that we are thinking about developing recreational-wise. I've got to leave in the morning. Go on up to the Canyon motel, get a hold of Don Demarest and he will show you around, see what you think.'

"Of course," Don said, "I had never met Louis. The next morning Louis, Kathy and the kids came driving in, we go up, look all over the ranch and this is what got Louis started there."

"Who was Bob?" Margaret asked.

"He was a land promoter."

"Does he live up there?"

"No, he lives in Pasadena. But had I not been able to get tickets for him that night, and if he had not sat at the table where Kathy and Louis were, we never would have gotten together. It's funny how things work out, you know."

Kathy had hamburgers and hot dogs with all the fixings ready. She helped us get settled and we started eating. What they say is true. Food cooked over a campfire and served in the open air tastes wonderful. She had bought Nutter Butter cookies, the current L'Amour family favorite, for dessert. As we finished eating I couldn't resist kicking the fire a little to hear it crackle.

Beau called our attention to a camp robber jay he spotted, saying where there is one, another usually shows up. And it did. "They will eat meat and cheese," he said, "and just about any food that is around."

Then Louis, Don and I went for a hike over to Taylor Lake, about a mile away. When we returned Beau told me how the camp robber jays came right up and helped themselves to some scraps.

After relaxing for a while we loaded our gear in the suburban. As we descended there was a lot of chatter, a story about cooling Don by slipping a snow ball down the back of his shirt. Beau was the whistler in our group.

From a distance we were able to see the lake where we had hiked. We passed the boilers we had seen on the way up.

Don said, "The story on those boilers, Reese."

"Yes?"

"They were all brought up on skids or sleds, with mules and horses pulling them up here. You can imagine in the old days. They had a couple of mills going here and after the thing closed down two of the more enterprising boys stayed behind, opened up their little still.

"They used the boilers to work their still and one night they consumed a little bit too much of their product and the whole thing caught on fire and burned down."

"When did they first bring them up here?" Margaret asked, as soon as she quit laughing.

"Oh, back in 1800. The pack rats and the tourists haven't been able to carry off those boilers."

There followed an informal colloquy between Kathy and Margaret about some early movie stars. Kathy had been an actress and knew many of them.

We stopped to make a search for wild raspberries. Angelique wanted her mother to go with her.

"I'm not going to get tangled in dumb old briers today," Kathy announced, climbing down out of the vehicle.

CHAPTER 6

ORDERING L'AMOUR BOOKS - 50,000 A CRACK

San Diego, California, that beautiful city near the Mexican border, was for a short time home to me. In November 1943 I completed midshipman training at Columbia University in New York City and was sent for further training to the Navy Torpedo School in San Diego.

About thirty-two years later Margaret and I were in Pasadena visiting her sister, Mrs. David (Georgine) Coleman. We planned to return to San Diego to see where I spent six weeks learning all about torpedoes — how they are launched, make their run to a target, and explode.

We were in touch with the L'Amours. So, when in the spring of 1975, Kathy found out we planned a side trip to San Diego, she told us we would have to include the San Diego Magazine and Book Agency on our itinerary.

The owner, Art Jacobs, was a good friend of the L'Amours. So Kathy set up a date for us to see him and get a tour of the distribution facility. A terrific organizer, Kathy usually made such arrangements for Louis, freeing him to write.

"We have been in I don't know how many book stores," I told her, "but have never seen the heart of a distribution center."

Margaret and I visited with Louis the day arrangements were being made. He was in the process of writing <u>To The Far Blue Mountains</u> and shared some of his plans for the remainder of the book.

"Why don't you put Icelanders in your books?" Margaret asked in jest. (Her four grandparents came from Iceland and she is unusually proud of this.)

"I have Icelanders in my books," Louis responded. "Well, actually I was thinking of having Icelandic in Barnabas's ancestry. I know quite a bit about Icelanders. My sister Edna taught school in Pembina County in North Dakota. She knew many there. They are smart people.

"I've been to Iceland twice in my wandering. Didn't really get into the country, though. My ship just went into port and left right away. Icelanders think they have a 'gift,' sixth sense, ESP or whatever. I need that in some future books I am planning about the Sacketts."

The San Diego I knew in 1943 was a quiet, small city where the navy's presence dominated the scene. I enjoyed my stay there, finding it rather relaxing after the rigorous midshipman training. In the intervening years the city had put runners out in all directions, with rapid population growth. When we found the large warehouse, Art Jacobs welcomed us warmly, treating us as if we were part of the L'Amour family.

His was not a small operation. At the time we visited his business, Mr. Jacobs had one hundred and three employees. His initial order of a new L'Amour paperback was 20,000 books, increasing to 50,000 as the years passed.[1]

"When our first order for one of Louis' new books arrives," Mr. Jacobs told us, "we immediately place a second order." I was amazed at that number of books handled by one distributor.

"We have 1200 accounts, of which eight hundred are book

---

[1] From a March 6, 1999 letter from Art Jocobs to the Citizens Stamp Advisory Committee in Washington, DC, to support a commemorative stamp for L'Amour.

stores," he explained. "We handle 180,000 TV Guides each week. Most of my business is in magazines and paperback books. This building has 63,000 square feet." Police dogs, trained by Mr. Jacobs himself, were kept on the premises.

Endless stacks of shipping cartons covered the floor of the receiving area. Mr. Jacobs pointed out a group of these stacked eight feet high on a large flat.

They contained L'Amour's latest book, a collection of short stories entitled <u>War Party</u>. The cartons were bound together with strapping tape. On the outside of one of the cartons was the cover of one of the books. Adjacent to this was plastered a big "TOP 10" sticker, indicating the latest of L'Amour's books to make the top 10 on a national best-seller list.

Next Mr. Jacobs showed us how retailers' returns are handled. First the covers are removed and returned to the publisher, then the coverless books are shredded.

We stood for several moments watching the process. I looked in vain for just one L'Amour book being tossed into the giant shredder. Not one.

In the January 19, 1978 issue of the *Wall Street Journal*, Earl C. Gottschalk Jr. wrote:

> Bantam expects to ship seven million L'Amour paperbacks this year, and to get few of them back. "There is a degree of absolute certainty in the sale of a L'Amour book," says Oscar Dystel, Bantam's president. "We often operate on the assumption that 45% of the books we send to bookstores will be returned; with Louis L'Amour the returns are usually about 12% — among the lowest in the publishing industry."

In my own experience the return of his books was less than that. We sold a large quantity of L'Amour books in our drug store in Jamestown. I can't recall ever having returned one to our distributor. Visiting with owners of a number of used book stores, I found very few are brought in for exchange. Most L'Amour readers save his books

In the same *Wall Street Journal* story, Mr. Gottschalk also stated:

In a publishing genre that has declined in popularity over the past decade, his [L'Amour's] sales keep climbing; he now accounts for about half the market for Westerns.

Mr. L'Amour long ago exceeded in sales such famous names as the late writers Zane Grey, a New York dentist, and Max Brand, who lacked Mr. L'Amour's thirst for authenticity. (Persuaded by his publisher to visit El Paso and soak up local color, Mr. Brand hated it so much that he locked himself in his hotel room and read Sophocles.)

Mr. L'Amour, now 68, has become one of the six best-selling living writers in any field, and is the biggest seller ever handled by Bantam Books Inc., having recently passed John Steinbeck. 'I guess I am an industry,' he says. So he is. But he also is a nonentity in Eastern literary circles. Despite a following of millions, his books usually are ignored by major reviewers, and it rankles. The westerns, he says, simply have been written off by reviewers.

Louis and I discussed this at length and he summed it up this way:

"If you write a book set in the past about something that happened east of the Mississippi, it's a historical novel. If you write about something that took place west of the Mississippi, its a Western — and somehow regarded as a lesser work. I write historical novels about the frontier."

After leaving Art Jacobs, I mulled over what I had seen. He had a smooth coordinated operation, the same as was required to place a meal before us aboard our destroyer in the Pacific.

When we stopped back at the L'Amours to say good-bye before heading back to North Dakota, Margaret said, "Louis, now don't forget to put Icelanders in your story."

"I did it," he replied. "I wrote it in yesterday."[2]

Later Mr. Jacobs and I exchanged letters. In response to my congratulatory note after Louis dedicated The Man From the Broken Hills to him, he wrote saying,

"Thank you very much for your very nice letter about Louis L'Amour dedicating a book to me. It was most thoughtful of you (and thank your wife for her greetings) and I appreciate your comments very much.

"As you know, Louis L'Amour and Kathy are two very special people who my wife and I feel are very much a part of our family. We love them both."

Louis and Kathy's family of friends was large. I recall when we joined them for a cook-out on the bank of the La Plata River in Colorado, another guest was their waitress from the Strater Hotel in Durango. That day it was Kathy who served her a hamburger.

---

[2] Last part of chapter eight in To The Far Blue Moutains. *Nial* is spelled *Njal* in Iceland. Njal's Saga is the famous old classic.

CHAPTER 7

SHOWING A YOUNG READER L'AMOUR'S NEW STUDY

In 1977 Matt Coleman, a young nephew of Margaret's who lived in Pasadena, had been reading L'Amour's books for years. I asked Louis if I could bring Matt over for a visit and his response was, "Oh sure." Kathy added, "Bring him for lunch tomorrow."

The next day, shortly after Margaret, Matt and I arrived at the L'Amour home in Beverly Hills, we gathered in the living room. Matt immediately spotted some of Shakespeare's books and asked Louis what he thought of him. There followed an intellectual discussion between the two about the works of this English writer and the theaters at the time. Margaret and I chose to remain silent. Our knowledge of Shakespeare and his works was a bit hazy.

Louis led us from their living room into the recently completed addition to their home. In the hallway an album of Charlie Daniel's was displayed on the wall. Matt stopped in front of it and asked, "You have an album of Charlie Daniels? I want to get one just like this to add to my collection. I see it's named *High Lonesome*. Isn't this the title of one of your books?"

"Yes, he has read my books for a long time and is a good friend. We have visited in each other's homes. We first met when his group was playing for one of Carter's Presidential Inaugural

Balls. He wanted to name this album *High Lonesome.* I told him
to go ahead. That was fine with me."

The following is on the back cover of the album:

To Louis L'Amour and James Bama[1]

Here's to gut-rotting whiskey and Saturday night
And pistols and poker and hellacious fights;
Here's to cowboys and trappers and mountains and woods
And "Slim With A Saddle" and "Rose Plenty Good";
Here's to hard-living men who took care of their own,
Like Chantry and Sackett, Catlow and Kilrone;
From the lowlands of Texas to high Tennessee,
What a hell of a fine place this world used to be.

My sincere appreciation for the hours of honest pleasure
you've both given me.

Charlie Daniels
1976

Then Louis led us into the recently completed area of his
house.
"Right here at these doors," he said, "is where the addition
starts. This area is known as the gallery. The bunch of books lying
on this chest just came in today."
We went in, moving down three steps.
Louis pulled out a drawer of one of his map cases. He told
us these were samples of a complete set of very detailed topographi-
cal maps of the entire United States.
Beginning with his early writing, the settings in which he
placed his characters were real. These maps were used to refresh

---

[1] Artist of the West.

his memory of the places he had been. Thus he gave his readers accurate accounts of the rivers, the mountains and the terrain where he placed his characters.

"This is a Navajo rug," L'Amour said, indicating one on the floor ahead of us. "I'll turn the corner over so you can see it properly. This line here is interesting, very interesting. It is the spirit train."

"I thought it might be a flaw," I said.

"No, it goes from the center to the edge. People used to think it was a flaw. It enables the weaver's creative spirit to escape from the rug so the weaver can keep on creating. Once in a while the weaver will decide this will be the last rug she will ever weave. So she weaves the train back into the rug, tying her spirit into it. Then she won't make any more."

The L'Amour collection of kachina figures was strikingly displayed on recessed glass shelves along one wall. Some call them dolls but Louis said this is wrong, they are spiritual figures. Most of his came from Colorado.

"This is a special and very precious piece," L'Amour said, showing us a Zuni altar.

"What is the figure?" Matt asked.

"It is the feathered serpent which figured in the religion of many of the American peoples."

L'Amour led us down more steps into his study. He called our attention to a very heavy wooden beam along the length of the ceiling.

Hanging on the wall above the fireplace was a painting of a man on horseback. I asked Louis if it was by William George.[2]

"Yeah, it's kind of a trial painting he made before doing the final."

"He has done the jacket paintings on several of your books, hasn't he?"

---

[2] One day when we arrived at the L'Amours we met William George. His finished painting of this subject appeared on the jacket of <u>Over on the Dry Side</u>.

"Yes," Louis said. "I like his work. He did the paintings for jackets on <u>To the Far Blue Mountains</u>, <u>Bendigo Shafter</u>, <u>Fair Blows the Wind</u> and some others."

Louis next showed us a painting entitled *Cradle Boy*. A baby boy nestled in a cradle on his mother's back. Straps over the mother's shoulders and under her arms held the cradle securely, freeing her hands.

We walked across another Navajo rug. Louis called it *Storm Pattern*. This was done by the daughter of the woman who made the one we saw near the entrance.

"This is a chair where I do a lot of reading," said Louis indicating an unusual antique chair. "This is a cock-fighting chair."

"A what?" asked Matt.

"Sitting on the chair as one normally would, they watched the cockfights in front of them and placed their bets here. These chairs were arranged around the pit where the cock fight was taking place." He added it was a marvelous chair to sit in and read.

"It can be used both ways. I prefer to straddle it because actually that is the most comfortable, with your back absolutely straight you see, and your book open in front of you. Like so. It's marvelous. I saw it in an antique shop. I was told it was made no later than 1810 and I believe this to be correct."

We now turned to his desk.

"My desk is four feet wide and eight feet long with no nails and no glue in it. It is hand carved and fitted, beautifully done, made of walnut. The man who made it had gone over to Spain and studied wood carving from an old man. He made these two side tables with four drawers, did all the carving himself."

I told Matt that Kathy L'Amour had taken Margaret and me over to meet the artist while he was working on the desk.

"Here is my pride and joy," said Louis turning to face a wall. "These double book shelves." They lined the walls. [3]

---

[3] The first hinged rows of high shelving could swing out, revealing a wall of books on shelving behind them. Louis used a sliding ladder to get to the high books.

He indicated a set of many volumes. "This is my complete history of the Civil War, all the official actual documents, reports from the fields, correspondence from the fields. One hundred and twenty-eight volumes. This is the bible on the Civil War. There is no place you can go beyond these volumes for an authority. This set was originally put out by the Federal Government around 1900. The originals are not in existence any longer.

"They only put out a few sets of it, so the National Historical Society, of which I am a member, decided to reprint it – if there was enough demand. They queried a number of people. I was one of them and we had to pay for it in advance. Then they printed – I think it was one thousand sets."

The Civil War was one of Matt's favorite interests, and he listened intently, wrapped up in what was being said.

Louis then described and showed us many of his books. They were arranged pretty much in categories.

He had a few novels. These were classics he had read in bygone days. He had accumulated thousands of volumes of non-fiction over many years, had read most of them, thoroughly skimmed the remainder. These books were his friends and he knew them well, just where each was on the shelf.

"I read mostly to remind myself," he told Matt in response to a question. "Because I have been over the terrain beforehand. I have scouted it all and know it very well. Then I go over it again from the books to make sure I was right. And I also read the memoirs of the people who went over the terrain."

Many times I have thought about what Louis showed us next.

"The last time I counted I had twenty-six stories started," he said. He quite often wrote two books at a time switching from one to the other. As he wrote he sometimes would think of an idea for another story, then write a few paragraphs, a few pages, or a chapter of it. These he would set aside to be finished at a later time.

He selected the beginnings of some of the twenty-six stories and read aloud to us:

"My name is Tatton Chantry and unless the gods untie the ropes I will die within minutes."

[Louis read this to us in February of 1977. In 1978 E.P. Dutton published <u>Fair Blows the Wind</u> which begins, "My name is Tatton Chantry and unless the gods are kind to rogues, I shall die within minutes." Later in 1978 Bantam published this in paperback and by 1988 there were fourteen printings.]

Let's look at another beginning Louis read to us.

"What I hoped for was a fat bear. What I came up with was a skinny Indian." This was to be a Sackett book about Kin Ring Sackett, the oldest son of Barnabas Sackett, whom his readers will remember from <u>Sackett's Land</u> and <u>To the Far Blue Mountains</u>.

The third of the twenty-six stories began,

"There stands a castle, well guarded and strong. This night I shall enter that castle. I shall scale the walls, open its doors of oak, walk down a silent hall with a sword in my left hand. In my left hand? I have no right hand."

This was to be a book about the first member of the Talon family. The Talons were early builders in America. They would build the bridges across the rivers, the steamboats that plied them and the railroads that stretched across the land.

As we left his study and went into the dining room, I knew a little more about where and how Louis spent so many hours of his life. Just as the creative spirit of the Navajo woman was seen in the rugs she wove, just as the craftsman's patience and exacting work were reflected in the desks he made, so did this writer create unique stories read and enjoyed by millions of people all over the world.

We were called for lunch. Kathy prepared and served the meal as easily and with the same enjoyable spirit Louis used in his writing. We sat on upholstered dining chairs in the bright and cheerful dining room, where she served us plates of hot dish, salad and rolls. The lively conversation was about movies, Beau's filming plans, Angelique's concerns about their dog, Spring, and Kathy's suggestion to Margaret that they go to a nursery to see about a cachepot.[4]

For dessert Kathy brought in a chocolate bundt cake on a tray. She cut and served it at the table, sprinkling powered sugar on each piece, then passed around the silver powdered sugar shaker.

"I made this cake for all you chocoholics," she said.

---

[4] A large flower pot.

50

CHAPTER 8

HEADING NORTH TO ALASKA - SITKA!

At times when reading L'Amour's stories, I do a bit of research on my own. This is true with reference to <u>Sitka</u>. I am thinking of two parallel areas of historical exploration.

While French fur traders and trappers paddled their canoes along the Great Lakes, Russian traders and trappers followed the rivers of Siberia to the Pacific. Perhaps we know more about the French and their activity than we do about the arrival of the Russians on the coast of Alaska. On his second voyage in 1741 a Russian, Vitus Jonassen Bering, was the first to explore the southern coast of Alaska. This newly discovered land became known as Russian America.

The treaty completing the negotiations on the purchase of Alaska from Russia passed our Senate on April 9, 1867. The agreed upon sale price was $7,200,000.

There is another treat in store for you who have not read <u>Sitka</u>. This story is one of L'Amour's best books and is appropriately dedicated to his wife, Kathy. It follows the story of Alaska from 1845 to 1867.

<u>Sitka</u> is one of Margaret's favorite L'Amour stories. There is romance here. This novel is steeped in events leading to the purchase of Alaska. L'Amour introduces us to his hero, Jean LaBarge,

who lived his early years in Pennsylvania. We move with him to the west coast and on to Alaska.

On one of the occasions when L'Amour and I were visiting in his study I was thinking about <u>Sitka</u>.

"In several of your books," I said, "you write about the sea. I like that because it reminds me of my experiences in the navy. Starting with <u>Sackett's Land</u> there are, among others, <u>Crossfire Trail</u>, <u>Fair Blows the Wind</u> and <u>Sitka</u>. Your knowledge of the sea and sailing vessels comes from your own experiences and this is reflected in what you write."

"You know," Louis said, "in <u>Sitka</u>, that was kind of fun. I actually got all the charts of that whole coast, the actual navigational charts, and laid out a course that the ship sailed. Every bit of it could be sailed just the way I wrote it.

"Now there is a scene where they transport the boat across a neck of land. This has been done too. I didn't realize how much at the time I wrote the story. I thought of this, you know, because I had this boat trapped up in an inlet . . . "

"I have wondered about this."

" . . . and there was a dense fog and a Russian gun boat was across the mouth of the inlet.

"Alaska at that time was possessed by the Russians. Though theoretically Americans could trade there, the Russian American Company wasn't allowing it. This was illegal.

"As soon as the fog lifted this gunboat was going to have my ship at its mercy. So what they did . . . they took it across this neck of land to the inlet on the other side and sailed away.

"When I thought of doing this I remembered this vaguely, having heard of a pirate down in the West Indies who did it. Two British warships had him trapped in a harbor and they were waiting for the sun to come up, for daylight to come. In the night he went over a neck of land and sailed away. When the sun came up he was gone, had vanished.

"So I began digging around for material and I found out not only had it been done that time but many other times. At one time they took a whole fleet of ships over a mountain to attack a fortress from behind.

"This fortress was in Italy on a lake shore. There was no access to the lake. The occupants of the fort never had thought of fortifying the lake side of the fortress very much, just the land side. The enemy got the idea of taking the ships over the mountain, launching them in the lake and attacking the fortress from behind. They did and it worked."

"That was a big portage, wasn't it?"

"That's right. They had to go much farther than I had them move overland in <u>Sitka</u>. All my navigation is correct, it all worked."

As I listened I recalled an excellent example of a portage of long ago. It is found in the story of the apostle Paul when he visited Corinth during his Second Missionary Journey. In the introduction of I Corinthians, <u>New International Version Study Bible</u>, there is a good description:

> The city of Corinth perched like a one-eyed Titan astride the narrow isthmus connecting the Greek mainland with the Peloponnese was one of the dominant commercial centers of the Hellenic World as early as the eighth century B. C. No city in Greece was more favorably situated for land and sea trade. With a high strong citadel at its back, it lay between the Saronic Gulf and the Ionian Sea and ports at Lechaion and Cenchrea. A diolkos or stone tramway for the overland transport of ships, linked the two seas.

"<u>Sitka</u> is very strongly historical," Louis continued. "I don't mention the ages of my heroes, Jean LaBarge and Rob Walker, because there actually was a little more spread in their ages than I implied. I had the boys together but actually Walker was a little bit older. But I don't say anywhere in the book how much older.

"Princess Helena Gagarin and her husband, Count Alexander Rotcheff, were real characters. There were many minor characters like Yankee Sullivan, with whom LaBarge had a fight in San Francisco, who was actually, in fact, the bareknuckle heavyweight champion of the world at one time. He was whipped in a saloon brawl by another man. Another character I used was run out of San Francisco by the vigilantes. I did a lot of research on that book, a lot of background. All the places in the book were real."

"It took you a good while to write that, didn't it?"

"Yes, it took me a while to write it. It took longer to research than actually write it because I started that one from scratch. Usually I write from a background of research I already have. In that case I didn't. What happened was this:

"I was asked by Darryl Zanuck to write a book. Darryl Zanuck at the time was running 20th Century Fox and he had great success with a book called Lloyd's of London. This was a case where a young boy, who later became one of the insurers at Lloyd's, had been a friend of another young boy who became Lord Nelson. As boys they had been friends together.

"It was a time when Lord Nelson needed desperately to keep his ships together, because they knew the battle of Trafalger was coming up. He didn't know it was going to be that battle but he knew there was going to be an opportunity to destroy the French fleet. He was watching for that.

"A number of insurers at Lloyd's wanted to have Nelson's ships taken away from him to protect their merchant ships at sea, to convoy them. So this one fellow who had been Nelson's friend as a boy fought desperately to keep the fleet in Nelson's hands. Their friendship changed the whole course of English history.

"So Zanuck wanted to do the same sort of story about American history. Knowing that I knew the field pretty well, he asked me if there was any such story. So I came up with two different ones, as a matter of fact. I haven't done the other one yet but I will.

"<u>Sitka</u> was the story of LaBarge and Walker and how it lead to the purchase of Alaska from Russia. Although Seward got the credit for the purchase, actually Walker was the one who really did the job.

"Walker[1] was a little wispy sort of a man, not quite five feet tall. He was a kind of Sam Rayburn type character or like Lyndon Johnson was before he became president, a smooth operator in the cloakrooms – the fellow who knew where the votes were and how to get them out. In this case it was even implied that Walker paid out about $200,000 in bribes because nobody wanted Alaska.

"They all thought it was a big boondoggle, a big waste of time. They weren't interested, you know, and it is implied he paid them just to get their interest, to get them involved because he wanted to get Alaska for our country.

"Walker was a guy – if it had been left up to him, we would have owned everything from the Panama Canal to the Bering Strait. He was the man who introduced the bill to recognize the independence of Texas. He introduced a bill to bring Texas into the States. He did most of the leg work to get the Oregon territory into the United States. He tried to buy a strip of Mexico twenty-five miles long below New Mexico and Arizona and all of Baja California. He made a deal with Mexico to buy it for $25,000,000. But it was an economy minded congress and they wouldn't ratify it."

"He had a vision, didn't he?" I asked.

"He really did. He was trying to create an enormous country here. He did all the leg work about Alaska and he was the one who was really more responsible than any other one man for the purchase of Alaska. No one believed in it but he himself."

---

[1] Robert J. Walker, an ardent expansionist, was a US Senator (1836-45).

CHAPTER 9

CONNECTING TO READERS
(And A Room Full of Gold)

"Because of the research, did it also take you a little longer to write <u>Sackett's Land</u>?" I asked.

"A little bit, yes," replied L'Amour.

"About the East Coast locale instead of the West."

"Yes, I was quite familiar with the East Coast locale and with England also, but I had to delve back into the history of England to some extent. I knew English history pretty well but my knowledge was more or less general. I had to pinpoint things to have them occur in a historical context.

"Now in my book, <u>To the Far Blue Mountains</u>, at one time they put a ship into Kinsale Harbor in Ireland at the time the Spanish were there. This actually took place. I had it worked right into that actual battle. It was really happening at the time. And wherever I can, I do this."

"In <u>To the Far Blue Mountains</u> did you have Barnabas finally settle in – I'm a little confused because in your book you couldn't name the place as it is today – was this in the Carolina area?"

"Yes, it was in the Carolinas."

"North Carolina?"

58

"Yes, the two sounds I mention are Albemarle and Pamlico Sounds. I took them up the river into the back country. Where I finally had them settle was in a place called Shooting Creek,[1] way up at the edge of the mountains. I chose it partly because of the name, I will admit, but also because of the locale. It was interesting there. They go over the mountain and the place where Barnabas is finally killed is up above Crab Orchard in Tennessee. Crab Orchard is quite a well-known place now – it's up in the mountains there."

"Have you finished your book that follows To the Far Blue Mountains?

"Not quite," L'Amour answered, indicating a neat stack of typewritten pages. "There it is on the desk right there. I am going to re-read it and see what I think of it now. I have let it sit for awhile."

"Do you do that quite often ?" I asked.

"No, I do that occasionally however. In this case I thought I would let it sit for awhile. It isn't quite what I had planned to have follow To the Far Blue Mountains. Nevertheless it fits very well and I think I will let it go. I am going to check it over. In the meantime, I've got another book which is almost finished."

"What's that?"

"I haven't got the title for it. But it is a Chantry story. The first Chantry."[2]

"This is finished?"

"No, it isn't finished yet, I will finish it in the next couple of weeks."

"I am in love with the Sacketts," I said. "But I am also interested in the Chantrys who have formal education. From them I have learned more about world history. Of course, there is a lot of history in Sackett's Land and To the Far Blue Mountains."

[1] See Chapter 14. In 1978 we met L'Amour in Chattanooga. One day we drove east on Highway 64 toward Franklin, NC. Shooting Creek was a green valley on the left.
[2] This story was published as Fair Blows the Wind.

"Yes there is, there is a lot of history in them. There are a lot of bits and pieces. You see that's one thing I deal with. I place all my stories in the context of the time. For example, I refer to the time when Shakespeare and a bunch of actors carried the Globe Theatre across the river. That was in <u>Sackett's Land.</u>

"That's a little bit of history lost to the general public. I thought they ought to know about it because it is kind of fun, kind of a fun episode that not many people know. Little things like that. Then, for example, in <u>To the Far Blue Mountains</u> that big cave at the end of Portland Island in England is really there. It is big enough for a sailing ship to sail into.

"When I got there during World War II, I started digging around for old papers, old books and whatnot. I found out about this cave and almost *nobody* in the town knew anything about it."

"Is that right?"

"I couldn't find a person in the whole town of Weymouth. Now, maybe I missed the right ones, but nobody I talked to had ever heard of such a thing. They kind of smiled very tolerantly at me when I mentioned it. They hadn't heard about it and who was this American coming in there asking about it? Finally, after quite a bit of trouble I got up on Portland Island and got to talking with one of the sheep ranchers. They raise a particular kind of blackface sheep that eat the salt grass and make very good mutton, with a special flavor.

"I was talking to him and he said, 'Well yeah, there's a hole of some kind out there in my pasture.' He had piled rocks around it and fenced it in so the sheep couldn't get into it. I went up there and looked down into it. I could see through a black opening down there to the green water below. So I took a newspaper I had, crumpled it up very roughly, set fire to it and dropped it into the hole. Burning as it went down, I could see a vast cavern, got a glimpse of it.

"I was at the time stationed there in Weymouth and one of my duties was giving hand-to-hand training to a bunch of commandos of the secret intelligence division. Commander Walker, of the navy, was in charge of it. I had a group from Africa, free French, some Australian and British Commandos. I was training a whole bunch.

"I told Walker about this so he suggested we get a navy assault boat and explore the thing. Well, in the book I had read, they said there were two passages leading off from this cave. At the head of one of them they found an old Roman sword lying on a kind of gravel beach at the end of the cavern. The other side had never been explored by anybody. We were going to explore it.

"I did get into the mouth of the cave. All our plans were made, everything was ready. Suddenly we got word the invasion was on. For a few days I was very busy shipping troops out from Weymouth, then I went over myself and that was the end of that.

"I haven't been back to Weymouth, but I intended to return. I am sure I will get some mail when this is published over there. I'll be curious to see what it is like."

"Are all your books published in England?"

"Yes, they automatically are published in England, as well as Australia and South Africa and some other English possessions, and in eighteen other languages.

"It's fascinating," Louis continued. "I find all kinds of little bits of history myself and I like to utilize these odd bits and pieces. I have taken a great deal of care in studying the countryside of England and also the conditions of the cities. I have studied London and some of the other cities, particularly the port of Bristol primarily because that was the most active seaport in England aside from London."

"In speaking to the group of writers the other evening I remember you were talking about never using a southern accent but using an expression." I remarked.

"I didn't mean a southern accent, but any accent."

"You are right, you didn't say 'southern,' I meant *any* accent."

"No. I don't believe in using any accent at all. It always sounds phony. No matter how you write it, you can never make it sound like the real thing does. So I try to pick the words, certain expressions to use. Now in To the Far Blue Ridge Mountains the expression 'I taken' is used quite a bit so I use that in my Sackett stories. And I will use other bits of phrasing. The way they put the words together implies what you want to convey, you see."

"I think you did a terrific job in To the Far Blue Mountains with the English language – the way a man from England at the time you write about would speak."

"Well, thank you," L'Amour quietly answered. "I try very much and I have a lot of books of the period. I read those also to try and catch the flavor of the thing. And of course Shakespeare is a help and so is Ben Jonson. At the time they were writing in poetical form. I have read Henry Fielding and some others."

"In making talks or speeches do you ever use the accent or brogue?"

"No, I never have tried that. They may come out once in a while but I never have purposely tried that. I use expressions or words to give the time and place."

"You are going to speak to a group of teachers in Hawaii. That's coming up in April, isn't it?" I asked. "What will be your subject?"

"Primarily they want me to talk a good deal about the West and my own experiences. I gave a talk for the California Association of Teachers of English a couple of years ago, out here near the airport at the Marriott Hotel. One of those fellows who heard me talk wanted me to speak to these teachers in Hawaii. He's on the committee and he asked me to give pretty much the same kind of talk I gave there. So, that's about what I will do.

"I will tell about the West, but I will also talk about where I got my material and how I handle the subject. That sort of thing."

"Are your requests for speeches increasing since you were on 60 Minutes?"

"Not just since then, but generally speaking over the whole period."

"Say in the last two years? "

"Yeah, I don't know actually how many requests are coming in now but Stuart Applebaum, who is public relations man at Bantam, says I could be speaking every single day if I would accept them. They weed them out for me. If something strikes them as being particularly interesting, they call me about it, we discuss it. But right now I am trying not to do anything until April first."

"Since you wrote <u>Sackett's Land</u> and <u>To The Far Blue Mountains</u> have you noticed any increase in mail from the East Coast?"

"Quite considerably, yes. The mail has picked up a lot. I have been getting good mail from England and I think we will get a lot more in the future.

"I had a very interesting thing happen after <u>Sackett's Land</u> came out. I got a letter from a fellow in England who lives right close to the Devil's Dyke. At the opening of <u>Sackett's Land,</u> Barnabas Sackett is walking on the Devil's Dyke and he slips and falls and finds this money there in the mud.

"So this fellow went out and took a photograph of the area where Barnabas was walking when that happened and sent it to me. He lives right close by. I like things like that. I get something like that every once in a while.

"It's a fun business if you do it the way I do. I enjoy it. I am doing the kind of work I like to do. It is fun to tell strange and odd little stories. The Chantry story I am doing now is going to touch on some things like that.

"He falls in love with a girl who is part Spanish and part Peruvian Inca. She is believed to know where there is a lot of treasure hidden – Inca treasure in Peru at the time their leader was murdered by the Conquistadors. A lot of this treasure had been headed toward Cuzco on pack trains of various kinds and when Atahuallpa was murdered they hid it all.

"The Spanish, led by Pizarro, had captured Atahuallpa and demanded a ransom for his freedom. For the ransom the Incas offered a room full of gold as high as a man could reach on a wall. [3]

"The Spanish agreed but while a lot of the gold was still in route they murdered Atahuallpa. So as soon as those bringing the gold found out Atahuallpa was murdered, they hid the gold right where they were and nobody has ever found any of it – at least supposedly they haven't. In my story my girl is supposed to know where some of this stuff is.

"Anyway, my protagonist helps her escape. It goes into a whole other story. So aside from my story of Chantry, the story of England, and the story of his landing on the coast of Carolina, I give you a good deal of the background of Peru and the Incas."

"This has been real interesting. I am going to let you rest for a while now. You have been talking for some time."

"O.K. Well, I've enjoyed it."

We took a short break. I got up and moved along the bookshelves, looking at the titles of his books. What stories each book would have if it could tell us through whose hands it had passed and of its influence on the lives of those who read it. Pausing to stretch, I noticed Louis pick up an item from his desk.

"What do you have there?" I asked.

"This is a fan letter I just received. I'll read it to you.

" 'I am from Wyoming. Both my husband and I are great

---

[3] The room full of gold was to be 22 feet long by 17 feet wide and 8 feet high. It would be once filled with gold objects, then twice filled with silver. Machu Picchu, John Hemming, Newsweek Book Division, 1981.

fans of yours. In fact we go out and, at times, end up buying the same book. We now have fifty-two of your paperback books and hope sometime we can get them all. We have four children and two of our oldest are even now reading your books and this has helped them in their reading at school.

" 'I guess what I am trying to say is we enjoy your books and would like to get more of them faster. I guess we will have to wait until they get here. Keep up the good work. God bless you and your family.' "

"Isn't that nice!" I said.

"Yeah."

"They don't expect an answer?"

"No."

"They just want to let you know they appreciate you."

"That's right. And that is typical of the letters I get. I get a lot of them that way you know. Here's another one from Spokane, Washington.

" 'I have been a long-time fan of yours. I felt compelled to write you concerning several of your recent books. Before I comment, my purpose in writing you is to discuss something else.

" 'I attended college at New Mexico Highland University in Las Vegas. While there I read you had a ranch in Mora, which is up the road from Las Vegas.' "

L'Amour paused to say, "I never did have a ranch there." Then he continued reading.

" 'For several weekends my roommate and I searched for your place in that area. We were never able to locate it. You see, we both wished to meet the man who held us enchanted with his understanding of not only the rapidly disappearing Western mode of life, but also of people and methods of dealing with adversity. There aren't many authors who grasp the full sociological process which greatly influenced our western heritage.

" 'My roommate and I wanted to talk to you, discuss areas in New Mexico and Arizona where we have lived which might provide material for your books and possibly listen to some of your stories. Our dream was never realized alas, but I continue to devour your books as they come on the market. I still look forward to meeting you some day and holding these long-desired discussions.

" 'To return to my intentions for writing you. I am currently taking some graduate courses in public administration. I work for the Veteran's Administration and part of our assigned reading material included work by Warren G. Bennis and Phillip E. Slater entitled <u>The Temporary Society</u>. This is basically a sociological theory on why democracy developed in America.

" 'In a section of this book the authors deal with something quite akin to your writing in that Slater believes the early settlers' children are more prepared to teach their parents about how to adapt to their environment than the other way around.

" 'In your books I have noticed an identical vein, particularly with reference to Barnabas Sackett and his offspring. The point may be moot, but I felt that [my] understanding in my current graduate study reading can only be attributed to what you have written and I thank you.

" 'I hope some day I will be able to attend a lecture you are giving, or meet you and talk. My roots are in the southwest and your literature helps me to continue my interest in the marvelous heritage no matter where I am.' "

"Louis," I said, "this is a good example where your writing has had a profound influence on the thinking of an individual."

"Yes, it is you know," commented Louis.

"If you had time this is the kind of letter that you would like to answer, isn't it?"

"That's right and I will answer this letter. I like to get letters like this where the reader finds my writing helps him in his field of study."

Louis placed this fan letter on top of several others and we left his study to see what Margaret, Kathy and the children were doing.

CHAPTER 10

UPHOLDING THE ORAL TRADITION

"What do you call this, Louis?" I asked. We were sitting in the new addition to L'Amour's house.

"Well, I usually call it the shack, but it is really my study. I should call it 'study.' It is a more dignified name."

I glanced around at book shelves containing thousands of his books. Louis picked one out and showed it to me.

"This is a register of a county in York that covers a period from 1556 to 1721."

"York?" I asked.

"Yeah, in England," he said. "And there are several baptisms here of Kathy's family. Baptisms, marriages and that sort of thing."

"Did you just get this book?"

"I've had it for quite a while but haven't had a chance to go through it. Actually, it is not a book you read, you know. It is just a list of baptisms, records and what not. I got it largely for that reason, because I knew some of her family was around there and I hoped we would find something of this in it."

"When we were in Culpeper, Virginia weren't we looking for something about her family?"

"Yes, but mostly about mine."

"I see."

"Mostly mine in Culpeper, but we found something about her family. Her family, so far as I know, was not in Virginia. They were in Arkansas, briefly in Alabama. One branch of the family was down in Texas and up in Montana. And one part of her family was completely lost in Texas.

"We don't know what happened to them. I haven't dug into it or done any serious research on it, but whenever I am reading anything about the area I always look for some sign of it, you know. I check every list I can find.

"They had a son who went off to the Civil War when he was about fifteen or sixteen, was fighting in the Confederate Army and it was reported he was dead. And either his family was killed by the Indians or moved away thinking he was dead.

"But he wasn't dead. He was only wounded and when he came back they were gone. He never could find any trace of them. After looking a while he gave up and went on out to Montana and became a mining man.

"I am not interested in books for their value," Louis continued, "only for their contents."

"You don't care whether It was published two weeks or five hundred years ago."

"That's right," he said. "I don't care as long as I have the information. If it was published five hundred years ago I would love to have it, but I don't care if it is the first edition or the twenty-fifth edition."

I told Louis I had a letter from Susan Gessner who is doing some graduate work on him and she is particularly interested in his relationship with his readers.

"She wants to know why you think such a personal relationship with your readers has evolved."

"That's a very interesting question. I don't know, but from all I have gathered, and from other writers and the writers I have read about, I think my relationship with my readers is much closer than any other writer, perhaps in history.

"I have established a very good rapport with them. I have had a chance through television, radio and autographing sessions to meet with a lot of them. So I have literally met face-to-face, for a brief period at least, with perhaps ten thousand of them, maybe more.

"Down in Tucson, for example, at one meeting I sold over three thousand books. I would suggest eight or nine hundred people came in there in the afternoon. Other places it runs all the way from fifty to four or five hundred."

"At these sessions you don't have much time to visit with each one, do you?"

"No. I can say "hello" and I usually . . . sometimes they say things to me which give me an inclination of what they are interested in or not interested in."

"You get a feeling, don't you?"

"Yes, I do. I get a feeling also for the type. And of course, occasionally there is a lull. Then I get a chance to talk for a while with someone, or someone will ask me a question and I will take time to answer.

"Then I get a large amount of mail, and in a surprising number of letters I find out the whole family is reading my books. Not just one member of the family — father, mother, son, and daughter — the whole outfit. This I like very much.

"When I am asked an intelligent question I try to answer it. My mail now has gotten completely out of hand. I can't answer it any more but I still try. I pin myself down to ten letters a week. I do write those ten letters a week."

"How many do you think you get, Louis?"

"Well, right now it is running from thirty to fifty. This week will fall a little bit low I think. I doubt if I get more than twenty this week. But sometimes it picks up, sometimes there is a big surge of writing. And every once in a while, of course, I get letters from people who have never read anything of mine at all when I go on television or something. They say, 'I'm going to read one of your books'.

"We have developed a nice relationship. Also they seem to identify with my characters, particularly the Sackett family. They haven't yet had a chance to get warmed up to the Chantry family and Talon family to the same degree. They know them but it is just a much shorter acquaintance so far."

"Well, you have written some fourteen or fifteen books about the Sacketts."

"Yes I have. I have written several books about Tell for example. They all feel very close to him. I am frequently asked when Tell is going to get married again. He was married once and his wife was murdered."

"I was with you in Cortez, Colorado when you were autographing in a book store there," I said. "I got the impression that all those who read your books feel like your characters live and, in a sense, you live in their minds because of these characters. Is that true?"

"I think this is probably true. They do seem to feel they live. Of course this makes me feel very happy, for this is what I am trying to do. Charles Dickens used to manage that very well and I don't think any writer since his time has done it quite as well as he did. He had them identifying with him very much.

"Readers are interested in my characters, but to get them really emotionally identified with them, you know, and feel warm toward them, is a whole different thing.

"I like my readers and they seem to like me. I write to please them."

"When did you first become aware of reader responses?" I

asked. "Or did you ever have this in mind?"

"Not to the extent that I do now. I first began to become aware of it when I got a letter from a Navajo sheep herder who was working over in Arizona. He was a young fellow who had gone to an Indian school, had some education.

"He and a friend were out herding, tending a flock of sheep and he was reading my book. Suddenly he realized that he was right on the spot where my story had taken place. I had been in that identical position and remembered it and had described it, you see. They got up, went outside, looked the area over, you know, to see what kind of job I had done. Then they wrote me a letter about it.

"This also was the thing that got me committed to writing about actual places," L'Amour continued. "Before that I had done it only occasionally in my short stories. So after that I decided to write about real places so the people could identify with them."

"Because they took the effort to write to you."

"That's right. And it helped a good deal. Ever since then I have tuned in closely to my readers' responses. Now, for example, I am fascinated with history and also with little bits of information. This sort of thing you know, tracking, trailing and living in the wilderness, getting along with nothing, surviving under bad circumstances.

"All these things have always fascinated me so I stick one of them in my stories every once in a while. I began to get a lot of reader response to that. People like it. So then I began to go heavy on that. So, in fact, I have learned from my readers."

"In other words, your readers aid you in writing."

"They really do, they really do. They have aided me a great deal, far more so than the critics perhaps. Few of the critics actually are familiar with my sort of material. They don't really know how to deal with it. They deal with it from the standpoint of other books they have known.

"But the people who write to me deal not from books, but from reality. They are dealing with life and the situations they have known and places they have been. Many of them know the places I have been to. They know the area. I get letters from people who say, 'Well, I used to punch cattle out in that area' or 'My father had a ranch down there and I know this place very well.'

"This is the sort of thing I like and these are the people I write for. I think that in these days with such a vast audience as you have, you have to pay strict attention to writing a story that will be absolutely authentic. Because, as I said before, somebody out there knows everything about what you are writing about. The audience of the size I have, you have to think about them all the time."

"Can you describe your typical reader?" I asked.

"No, there isn't a typical reader. I have had letters from people whose age is from nine to ninety-four and all the ages in between and from every level of intelligence, from people who could barely write to the most intellectual people in the country, from many many teachers, from professors in college.

"Many, many scholars in all different areas are fans of mine. I have many fans in the state department, in the justice department, many senators and congressmen read my work. Many in the army and navy. There is no typical reader with the exception that they do have a conditioned response, you might say, or at least a warmth for any regard for American history.

"They are fascinated by history and their country. This is one thing we have in common. They are interested and they have come to know over the years that I know what I am talking about. Not because I am any super intellect but simply because I have had the time to pursue the question and read a lot of the books they haven't yet had the time to read and may never have the time to read."

"I know," I said. "Over the years I have mailed your books

from my drug store to many total strangers. It never entered my mind that I wouldn't be paid for the books. I have always been paid by return mail."

"Uh huh".

"I think this reflects the honesty you find in people who read your books. They are a down-to-earth type of people."

"Yes, they are. I have often said that if I had to populate a new country, I would like to do it with my readers. It's not because they read my books, it's because they are generally such nice people, good people. And when I autograph books for them, sometimes I get a chance to talk with this one or that one a little bit. Overall they are very solid citizens."

"From time to time I have been here when you open your mail," I said. "I know how much you appreciate these letters from your readers. Certainly the fact you can't answer them all doesn't mean that you don't want to hear from them."

"That's right, I like to hear from them and I am going to answer all I can. Yes, they are very important to me. It's not an ego thing at all, it's a companionable thing, an interchange, interchange of ideas, you know. They are telling me what they are thinking about, their response to my books.

"For example, one of the reasons why I have enlarged on the family idea, the three families – I intended to do it, as you know, had it in the back of my mind always but I hadn't really convinced myself nor my publisher that this was the way to go. Until letters began to come in. 'Why don't you write a book about Parmalee?' He is one of the Sacketts I have mentioned a couple of times in my stories but I haven't written about. Then I get letters coming in, 'What about Joe Sackett? You've never mentioned him any more, or Bob. What happened to them?' They were the younger brothers of Tell and Tyrel and they have kind of fallen by the way, you know."

"Do you know," I asked, "of anyone else who is interested in writing about you and your relationship with your readers, other than Miss Gessner who is doing this at the University of North Dakota?"

"Not at this time, no – I am thinking of other topics. One fellow is doing a paper now on my handling of the American family and how the family figures in my stories. And I think I am one of the few people who is dealing with that subject to any extent now. Most people's thinking regarding the family is that it is a dead concept.

"I don't think so at all," L'Amour continued. "I feel it is stronger than it ever was. It is going through a difficult time right now and there are various things that are making it less viable than it used to be. It used to be that the family had to be together to share the work, share the living and that was the only way they could get along.

"Now it is no longer true. But there still is a big emotional thing that they share, an intellectual thing. We have it in my own family. We have a very free exchange of ideas here and we all read, we all talk, we all think about things. We all have opinions."

"From time to time you have met some of your readers. I am thinking about Val Wirth who lives in Australia. You bring her into your home and you entertain her here. Why don't you closet yourself?"

"Well most writers do but I don't. In the first place I like people. I enjoy them and I enjoy meeting them. Here was a lady who lived in Australia, she is a librarian down there, has access to all kind of information. She has a very good education, good background and she wrote me about my work.

"When I responded an exchange grew up and she finally said she wanted to come to the US to see some of it. So when she did we showed her around. I was glad to have the opportunity. I would enjoy it in more cases.

"Every year, you know, I go to Colorado in August and somehow this has been noised about, partly by word of mouth, partly by comment I have made on television. People ask me and I tell 'em how we go out there, about sleeping all night in one of the Cliff Dwellings and this sort of thing.

"So now it's gotten so that every summer people show up there looking for me. Last year nearly one hundred came and said that was their purpose. Some of them I made contact with and some of 'em I missed."

"In a sense, this is sort of a modern day nail keg, cracker barrel group, isn't it?" I asked.

"Yes it is."

"That you like to sit down and visit with."

"I consider myself a storyteller, not an author or novelist, but a storyteller in the old oral tradition of storytelling. You know Homer when he told the stories of Iliad and the Odyssey. Homer went around to various castles and homes and places and into Greece and told these stories. He was a blind poet. He sang these stories and poetry.

"This was the way for thousands of years in the world. There were storytellers, most of them professional, some amateurs, who just drifted around the country telling stories. Wandering minstrels you know, in the marketplaces of Asia. There were men who sat down in the corner of the marketplace and told stories – story collections.   That's how the Arabian Nights originated and there is another great collection called the Ocean of Stories.

"This is the tradition of which I think myself. I am one of the old oral storytellers. I don't want them to think of me as an author. I am a storyteller, I communicate directly with people. The book just happens to be the medium."

"There is no question about your having been very successful in your storytelling," I said. "Most people like to know, well, it's a private thing in a sense, but they like to know how many books you have sold and things like that. I don't think they are trying to figure out your income. I think they are just interested to know how many other people are reading your stories."

"Well, at this point, in eighteen languages I have sold seventy million books. That's at the end of this past year, 1976."

"Does this include those published by Fawcett?"

"This is Fawcett, and Bantam – and a small number with Ace just before that. Most of the sales of course are with Bantam. They entertained me in New York recently with a big party to celebrate my fifty million sales with them. And the other twenty million are Fawcett, Ace, and foreign sales.

"Wasn't it just about fifteen months ago that they celebrated forty million sales?"

"Yes."

"So, since then, ten million."

"Uh huh. It's mounting up very fast. Every year it's growing and every year I am meeting more people."[1]

"Louis, do you have any idea about, say, the average number of days a year you spend on touring, television appearances, etc.? What portion of your time?"

"I would say in my biggest year not more than one-tenth of my time. There are spots, lectures, discussions here and there – like the other evening, this book affair where we were. I do things like that, you know, but they don't take me out of my work very much. Just for a very short time. These give me some outside contact which I enjoy. But I go on a tour, usually not more than three weeks in a year, where I will hit a number of towns."

"In connection with that, what cities or parts of the country are typical? Do you cover the same area?"

"Well, no, it varies considerably. I've covered every area

---

[1] By the year 2000 sales had passed 300,000,000.

except New England. On a typical tour I'll hit Cincinnati, Cleveland, Chicago, Nashville, Atlanta and perhaps Dallas and Fort Worth. It varies a good deal.

"I have been in Dallas and Fort Worth several times as a matter of fact, partly because of the demand for me there and Houston, and partly because I was there actually doing some work on a movie."

"Another reader of yours, Gene Hoffman, from Tennessee inquired about your early work when you wrote Hopalong Cassidy stories. He wanted me to ask you if they will ever be bringing them back in paperback."

"I doubt it very much. Hopalong Cassidy stories were created and developed by Clarence E. Mulford and I had nothing to do with them until at the close of his career when suddenly Bill Boyd and Hopalong Cassidy movies got on television. Before that they had been completely dead, you see. Then they got on television and there was a big boom business in Hopalong Cassidy.

"So an eastern publisher decided there was a demand for books, so he went to Mulford who was seventy years old. He was up in Maine and was fishing. He had made his money, he was happy, he didn't want to be bothered.

"So they – I believe from what I heard, they asked him if someone else was going to write the movie whom he would prefer. They were to pay so much money, of course, for doing it. He named three names and I was one of them. I was the one they chose.

"They paid me a flat price to write these four books. A flat price for each one of them and I get no royalties from them whatsoever. I have no interest in promoting 'em.

"The stories were mine only in the sense I took his characters and created the stories around them. I was very familiar with his stories and I always liked them. I wanted to write about the original Hopalong Cassidy he wrote about. His Hopalong was nothing like the Bill Boyd character of Hopalong.

"Hopalong got his name because he had been shot in the knee at one time and he limped a little bit. So they called him Hopalong. But he also was a red headed, tobacco chewing, rye drinking, poker playing cowboy. He was more or less a typical cow puncher only he happened to be very good with a gun. I wanted to take him and write about him and they agreed that I could. Then after I had signed the contract with them, they reneged on that and wanted me to use the Bill Boyd character.

"Well, I needed money. This was early in my career, and I struck a very bad time. I had come back from the war and had started from scratch and built a place for myself writing for pulp magazines. I was branching out into slick magazines and getting these other things with the intention of going on, when all of a sudden and overnight the pulps died you see. Almost in a matter of thirty to sixty days they disappeared. From making a fairly reasonable income suddenly overnight it was gone – just like snow on the face of the desert – wham!

"It disappeared and I literally had no where to go, yet I had bills to pay like everybody. And in this hiatus they stepped in with this offer for the books on Hopalong Cassidy. So, what I did, I took some of the old Hopalong novels and went back over them and picked out some character Mulford had used and dropped some minor character in the story.

"For example there was one fellow that left the ranch and went off and started a ranch of his own. So, I decided to have this man get into trouble and then have him send for Hopalong to bail him out. I built my story around that. So I wove my stories right into the fabric of the Mulford stories in such a way as they would seem to be his. I even got two or three reviews saying these were better than the original Hopalong series. But anyway I did four of them and they are off the market, forgotten."

"For those serious readers," I said, "who are making a study of your work, I think there would still be copies of these books in libraries. I know the Jamestown, North Dakota library has some of the Hopalong books."[2]

"I didn't know there were any of them still around, but I am glad they have a few of them anyway."

---

[2] Some of the Hopalong stories have been recently published by Bantam.

L'Amour enters old cabin along the LaPlata River near Durango, CO. He writes about this in his book <u>The Quick and the Dead</u>.

Don Demarest and Louis L'Amour in the Cumberland Mountains in Colorado. Don lives in Hesperus, CO, was location scout for movie studios. Don came West from New Jersey.

Angelique at home with Spring.

Kathy and Meredith at luncheon reception for the L'Amours in Greenville, SC. 1975.

Orien McCallister and Reese's two uncles, Cody Hawkins and Jake Morgan, watch as Beau L'Amour aims at target before pulling the trigger. They are at the Hawkins old homeplace, Greer, SC. 1975.

Bob Gillespie at his home near Hendersonville, NC cradles a Gillespie Rifle manufactured by one of his ancestors during early settlement of our country. 1978.

L'Amour's party for Val Wirth, librarian from Australia.
Margaret serves herself stuffed grape leaves. Val visits with
actress, Susan Brown, a longtime friend of Kathy L'Amour.

**Val visits
with Louis.**

Reese and Louis at his home in Los Angeles in 1975. Photo by Carol Lee Veitch, longtime friend of Kathy L'Amour.

Reese enjoying the large cache of L'Amour books at Art Jacob's Distribution Center in San Diego. These titles extend off to the right of the picture for some distance.

Entrance to the new addition to L'Amour's home in Los Angeles. His study is ahead and angles to the right.

Louis at his desk in his study.

L'Amour honors pioneers as he gives address to those attending the Ground Breaking Ceremony of North Dakota Heritage Center in Bismarck. Govenor and Mrs. Arthur Link.

Cameras click as Louis breaks the native sod. Reese Hawkins (center with back to camera) sees the job well done.

Reese, Louis, Taresa Hawkins in carriage, Ann Stephan (Bismarck), Sigga Benson, Margaret Hawkins (Jamestown), Eve Schultz (Bismarck). Group in background finishing lunch served from chuck wagon.

Allan Hawkins put down his camera to check daughter in carriage. Margaret and Sigga Benson (Bottineau).

Louis autographing one of his books in Bismarck for Ernest Young of Jamestown. 1976.

Bob Melland of Jamestown, Master of Ceremonies for Ground Breaking Activities, meets Louis before program starts at site of the planned North Dakota Heritage Center. Tom Clifford (center) and Kent Jones look on.

Reese takes picture of Margaret and Louis as their plans for the day are tape recorded during breakfast at the famous Read House in Chattanooga, TN.

Reese and granddaughters, Tamarie and Taresa Hawkins, next to the tour bus on one of its stops. Knoxville, TN, 1980.

As they look at Shooting Creek, Louis tells Reese why he had Barnabas Sackett choose this location for his home in the beautiful Blue Ridge Mountains. Louis' frontier story, <u>To The Far Blue Mountains</u>, is about the beginning of the Sackett family in America. This was "the West" to the Europeans at that time.

Louis meets knowledgeable Emily Kemmer who lives across the road from their country store. Margaret listens and learns. 1978.

Two great story tellers. Les Hill, department store owner in Crossville, TN and Louis have just met. This hospitable host was the guide for the three of us for several hours.

In 1998 after twenty years the Hawkinses returned to Grassy Cove where they visited with Emily Kemmer. Emily (on right) and Carol Smith sit in rocking chairs by the black potbelly stove.

Prescription written in 1912 by L'Amour's veterinarian father, Dr. L.C. LaMoore.

Lieutenant Ambrose Freeman was Louis L'Amour's great-grandfather. This picture was taken by Reese Hawkins in 1976 about ten miles north of Tappen, ND near where the Battle of Big Mound took place. Freeman was with the Sibley Command.

President Reagan presents The Congressional Gold Medal to L'Amour, September 24, 1983. Rodeo contestants witness the event.

Kathy and Louis before he receives an honorary doctorate from North Dakota State University, Fargo.

L'Amour signs book for Crossville customer. Bookstore owner
Patricia Kirkeminde looks on. Reese's recorder in foreground.

Painting of
Theodore
Roosevelt Rough
Rider award
winner, Louis
L'Amour. This
oil on canvas by
North Dakotan,
Vern Skaug,
hangs among
other award
winners in the
State Capitol,
Bismarck, ND.

James Troutman, Margaret, Reese, Kathy, Wayne Sanstead, Jake Wolf, Pastor Herb Flitton at the Louis L'Amour school dedication. September 1990.

The Hawkinses are guests of the L'Amours for lunch at the Parker Meridian Hotel, New York City 1985. Photo by Meredith Hawkins Wallin.

CHAPTER 11

USING AN ALIAS

It was February of 1977. L'Amour and I sat in his study. There was no campfire, but as I listened, I could visualize glowing coals casting moving shadows on Louis' face. He paused to sip the coffee he had poured from a white pitcher-shaped thermos.

Coffee was to a North Dakotan as buttermilk was to my grandparents who lived on a farm near Greer, South Carolina. I recall my grandmother sitting on an old straight-backed cane chair in a corner behind their wood burning stove. With her right hand she moved the dasher of a large churn up and down; with her left she turned the pages of a book.

Later, during World War II, what a comforting feeling it was to hold a hot cup of coffee while on early morning watch on the bridge of the destroyer. As I'd matured and my horizons widened, my craving for a glass of cool buttermilk had changed to one for a cup of hot coffee.

Now, when I'm reading one of L'Amour's books and his characters are drinking coffee out of a tin cup, I get up and go to the kitchen for some of my own. Sipping my coffee, I continue reading and once again become an unseen character in his story.

"Louis," I said during a pause, "you mentioned you had started a story based on your life."

"Yes, I have. A number of people wanted me to write my autobiography and I think that I should because nobody else knows the facts. There isn't anyone in a position to get the facts. Of my period since I have been writing, yes, that's pretty much public knowledge or at least a lot of it is. Not my personal reaction to it, but otherwise.

"For example, when I went to sea, I very rarely went to sea under my own name. This was due to a variety of circumstances. When I'd first got a chance to go to sea, I had been boxing under another name. Everybody knew me under that name."

"I see."

"So, had I switched to another name, they would have begun to wonder what the score was. So I just went ahead with the name I had been boxing under.

"And later on another trip to sea, I was wanting to go to sea and I had lost my seaman's papers. A friend of mine had got a job on a ship and there was a job for me also. But I had no able seaman's ticket. It so happened he had one, he had an extra able seaman's ticket. He had loaned a fellow some money on it, you see. So I went to sea, made a trip around the world under another fellow's name."

"This was a different time," I said. "But even then Louis, you could have died and no one would ever have known . . ."

"That's right."

". . . known what happened to you."

"No one would have known at all, particularly under the circumstances which that trip began. I was in San Pedro and my family knew I was there. I had written to them a number of times. I was looking for a job and there weren't any jobs available. Very bad times.

"There were some six hundred seamen on the beach at San Pedro alone and they were all broke and were all looking for a job.

I ran into this fellow one night at the Seamen's Institute. It was a kind of a place run by the churches, something like a Seamen's YMCA. I was there one night and I got to talking to a fellow near the fireplace. He told me there had been a radio call for a couple of seamen. He was going to meet this ship that was to come in at two o'clock in the morning to take on fuel. There were three men actually, one man in the black gang, that's the engine department, one a steward in the mess department and a seaman. He suggested I come along. There might be a job there for me too. So I went along and that was when I used this other able seaman ticket. One day, I had been there around town and then I vanished! There was no record of my going."

"Right."

"You see, my family tried to locate me and couldn't because the next time they heard from me I was in Yokohama, Japan."

"That was weeks later, wasn't it? "

"Yes. That was quite a while. And so, I could really be vanished off the face of the earth – for a short time. And there were other periods like this and then for a while when I was living in Oklahoma. I was living there trying to get started writing. My folks had moved there. I was living with them part of the time. Every once in awhile I would leave there and go some place out of the area and fight, usually under another name because at the time I wasn't training very well. I wasn't thinking about fighting regularly and I didn't want to take a beating under my own name."

"Uh huh."

"As a matter of fact I didn't lose many fights. I lost only five altogether but during this time I didn't lose any. But nevertheless, I went to sea a couple of times from there. As far as anyone in the area knew, I was out on the farm with my folks. As a matter of fact I had gone off and worked for a couple or three months.

"Then I would show up again but no one knew me well

enough to be curious or anything. I had no intimate friends and it wasn't until after I began training some boys to box that I got acquainted with people in the area."

"This book, are you going to write it as another person but base it on your life?"

"I am writing it as fiction, using another name. It is going to be my life's story, almost entirely true. Naturally, I am going to have to try to remember the dialogue, that sort of thing. That is one reason I am writing it as fiction. You see my experiences are totally different from the usual experiences. Though there were a lot of others who had similar experiences.

"At the time I was knocking around there were a lot of soldiers of fortune and drifters all over the world. They were living by their wits, living any way they could get along.

"In Shanghai, China, for example, where I was for a short time, there were perhaps two or three thousand soldiers of fortune with no allegiances, mostly with educated backgrounds, mostly from good families. Not all, but mostly. They were just drifting like I was at the time, just took whatever came to hand. I had what might be called a very adventurous life, but it wasn't intentionally so. I had always wanted to have that kind of life."

"You didn't plan those years?" I asked.

"No, *they happened.* I just took advantage of what happened . . ."

"Some young people," I said, "want to canoe down the Mississippi River."

"Yeah, well this I had always wanted to do – not to canoe down the Mississippi River – I had always wanted to travel. This is the way I did travel. When it happened, it happened by accident. I just followed the main chance you might say.

"For example, this fellow in San Pedro that night. He suggested I might get a chance to – I had always wanted to go to the far east – he suggested I might go on this ship. So I went. I might just as easily have said no. But I didn't. I went down there and so I got the chance. Just one thing led to another. The opportunity was there.

"I was broke in Surabaja, in Java. I had been there a couple of days, had a little money left but not much. I ran into a guy on the waterfront there that I had met briefly in New Orleans several years before. He asked me what I was doing. I told him I was just drifting, looking for something to do. He said, 'Look, we need a second mate in cargo.' I said, 'I don't have a ticket.' He said, 'Well you don't need one, it's a sailing vessel. You only need two tickets on a sailing vessel. The captain and I each have one.'

"So, I went along. I was with them for a year. We went all through Indonesia. At the time I was there it was the East Indies. Borneo, Java, Sumatra.

"The man was captain of the ship, and owner of the ship also I might say. It was a three masted auxiliary schooner. The man I was working with was sixty-five years old at the time. He had been in Indonesia in those waters since he was fifteen years old. In other words he had been fifty years down there and had seen all that country. Having the kind of vessel we had and trading the way he did, the only way he could make money was to go into all of the smaller ports and the out-of-the-way islands and places where nobody else could really afford to go.

"Somebody on a regular line, they figure well that's about three hundred miles, it is out of my way. There is no reason for me to go up there for that amount of cargo. They wouldn't do it but we would. Our captain, having a sailing ship, could afford to because he only needed the wind. And so, he had gotten around an awful lot. I not only profited by my experience on that vessel but I profited by his fifty years experience.

"He used to come up and be with me sometimes at night,

partly because he liked to talk, partly because after all I wasn't an officer and I had had some experience at sea. Perhaps he wanted to keep an eye on things to make sure I was doing all right. But we would talk there and sometimes he would spend an hour or an hour-and-a-half with me up there during a four hour watch.

"He talked, reminisced about his days. He had been there when a lot of *black birding* was going on. This was when a ship used to pull into a little island, some of the natives would come aboard and then the ship would sail off to sea and sell them as contract labor. It wasn't really slavery, it was almost that."

"What a story!" I said.

"They were being paid a pittance, these people were, but they didn't want to go in most cases. He was down there when that sort of thing was taking place and when a lot of raiding of pearl fisheries was going on. First it wasn't important because you could fish pearls anywhere but then later they set up reserves. You could fish in them only certain times a year and he had been down there when a lot was happening, had been involved in a lot of it.

"There were a lot of native wars. Indonesia is now one country, but in those days it was many different countries. There have always been pirates down there. There are pirates down there right now.

"Now they use motorized sampans, dugout canoes with outboard motors and five or six of these working in a group. Sometimes fifteen or twenty will suddenly come and raid a village or town on the sea coast, loot the town completely and sail away. Many of these pirates live in Palawan in the Philippines and raid down the coast of Borneo.

"This is still going on right today, but over here you don't think of that sort of thing. Unless you are tuned to that background and know what is happening, you don't dream there is any piracy today. Yet there is, there is also piracy in the Red Sea. This sort of thing was going on then and I had the benefit of my skipper's fifty years experience and all the stories he was telling me."

Louis said he used to copy down the various sailing directions from the log book. What direction you would use sailing into a harbor, etc.

"Many of my early stories were about that area," he continued. "I wrote a story called *Night Over the Solomons* that appeared in a pulp magazine about a troop transport that was sunk off the coast of Kolombangara. One man got ashore only to discover the Japanese had built a base there. They were bringing their supply ships into this little harbor which was completely concealed unless you flew right over it. They had cleared the trees off the space between the two mountain bases and made an airfield out of it where they could land planes. They were doing this to attack the troops on Guadalcanal."

The phone rang. L'Amour answered it, spoke briefly, then turned back to me.

"Kathy is inviting you for dinner. She is saying you might want to go with her. She's going to go to the market and pick up some things."

"That's fine, I would like that."

"But anyway, to get back to this story," continued L'Amour.

"I don't want it to end because its too fascinating."

"Well, I was telling about this landing field. This was a conception of mine. Shortly after my story was published and I am sure it had no connection. I am positive, no connection. The American navy went there and pounded the Japanese base right where I had imagined it might be."

"Isn't that something?"

"Well, really, it is logical. Because I looked around and thought, well supposing I were a Japanese and wanted to attack the supply ships that were going to Guadalcanal. Where would I do it?

I began to think of this place I had been, a perfectly hidden base."

"Do you think someone may have read your story?"

"I doubt it. But here is another interesting thing. At almost that same time a few miles off the shore of Kolombangara Island, a young man who later became President Kennedy was shipwrecked. The man in my story was shipwrecked on one of the several inlets off the coast of Kolombangara about twelve miles away – almost the same time.

"I have written a lot about that part of the world. Actually my second published story was laid in the East Indies. I wrote a whole series of stories about a character named Pongo Jim Mayo, who was the captain of a tramp freighter operating in the East Indies before and at the beginning of World War II. I used the name Jim Mayo for myself for a while.

"I had a publisher for a brief time who didn't believe anyone would read a western by the name of Louis L'Amour. So they insisted I use another name.

"So thinking of no other name at the moment, I used Jim Mayo. I wrote a series of stories that were published in pulp magazines."

"What is the difference between pulp and slick?" I asked. "I guess slick is a little more expensive in appearance."

"Yes, and different kind of paper. In those days they were differentiated by their paper. The pulp magazines were published on wood pulp paper."

"Louis, I'll bet you I read some of your early stories."

"You could have. There was a time hardly a month went by when I didn't have two or three stories in the stands at once."

CHAPTER 12

SPEAKING TO INDIANS
WHAT'S THIS WHITE MAN DOING HERE?

"We have just returned from an Indian School where you spoke to a group of students," I began. "How did this come about?" Louis and I were visiting in his study in 1977.

"Well, I have a friend who is a Ponca Indian chief. He's an Indian who has worked in pictures. Actually he is called a Ponca-Sioux.

"The Poncas were a relative of the Sioux but not closely attached. In fact, the Sioux gave them a lot of trouble at various times. The Ponca lived back in the area roughly between Omaha, Nebraska and Sioux Falls most of the time. For a short time they were also in Pipestone, Minnesota.

"Anyway, I have known Chief for some little time, talked to him when he is in the area. He played the part of an Indian in *Shalako*, one of my pictures. He is a marvelous bareback rider and a very interesting man in his own way. From time to time I have gotten bits of information from him about the Indian. He knows a great deal but it is not always easy to get it out of him.

"He asked me if I wouldn't come down to speak to this group of Indians. As it happened the Indians had had a very difficult time in school because both the Blacks and Chicanos had beaten up on them, abused them and they are very much a minority . . . a very minority minority. So they'd established this school at the Indian Center called the Refugee School. They are literally refugees from other schools."

"Oh I see."

"They are a scattering of Indian children of various tribes and they are doing their best to give them some kind of education there. They asked me if I wouldn't come over and speak to them.

"Well, it was very difficult for me because I didn't know of any focus of interest for them. I tried speaking in general about Indians and some of the Indians who had succeeded in life. And this, I think, is important for the young Indian to realize.

"I don't want him to feel he is boxed in by our society. I want them to feel there is an opportunity out there for them and many Indians have succeeded in our society, but unhappily or happily, as the case may be, they mostly have Anglo names so they aren't thought of as being Indians.

"One I did mention was Thomas Gilcrease who established the Gilcrease Museum in Tulsa. He made a huge fortune and spent it very wisely and established the museum. It is a very lovely place."

Louis also told them about a leader at Phillips 66 Oil Company and Charles Curtis who was Vice President of the United States.

"In your talk, did I hear you mention 'belly dancers' when you were talking to them?"

"Yes, ballet."

"Oh, 'ballet'." I chuckled a bit.

"Yes. I hope I didn't – I remember now, I said that, kind of slurred over it a little bit. No, Maria and Marjorie Tollchief were two of the finest ballet dancers of our time. Marjorie particularly."

Louis mentioned several other well known Indian dancers.

"I think it is important that these young Indians realize that other Indians have made it and it can be done, so they have some model, something to shoot at. Too often they feel they are boxed in by our culture and there is no place for them to go. They are trapped."

"Most of us have our heroes," I said, "and if they knew about some of their own who have done so well, they would also have their heroes."

"That's right! They need their heroes. They need their heroes and then they can say, 'If he could do it, I can do it', you see. That's the idea I would like to convey. So I told them about that and a few other things but it was – while their eyes were focused on me and I knew I had their attention, I didn't know in what direction their interest went.

"I chopped around a little bit, touching this spot and that spot hoping I would get some response, but there wasn't any visual response. Probably there was a lot but you couldn't tell it.

"I finally got a question or two. William Crow, their teacher, asked about Crazy Horse. You see when you get a question or two you can enlarge upon it. I went ahead and told about Crazy Horse and about how his tactics are studied in many military academies around the world, how important they were.

"There are a lot of such items I could enlarge upon if I knew where their interests lay. This would give me something to play off on. If I would speak to them five or six times, I am sure I could contribute a great deal. It would have been difficult for the first two or three times."

"Yes."

"But then I think we would start getting together and they would warm up to me. You see, after all, I was a stranger and a white man."

"That's right."

"And what is a white man doing talking about Indians? That's the first thing they are going to think about."

"True."

"Then I would say several things that they obviously were not sympathetic to. Unhappily, a lot of the ideas the Indian has he got from the white man. And one of them he got from the white man is the story about Custer. While he fought the Indian, Custer's sympathy was very much with the Indian."

"That's interesting."

"He fought them because they were on the warpath. They had to be put down, they had to be stopped and brought into a reservation. But his sympathy was with them completely. And he tried again to help them and he got himself in trouble over it."

"Isn't it very difficult to speak to a group like this, Louis?"

"It's extremely difficult to speak to them because, you see, I'm not a speaker who uses any kind of set speech. If I did I would just go up there and say it and 'to hell with the audience' you might say.

"I respond to my audience. When I start talking, I watch their faces and from them I get an indication of where their interests lie. I go in that direction and then also try to add a little bit to their knowledge. It is nice to know where their interests lie and what they want to know. I have a lot to tell people and I am anxious to deliver it but I want to ask them what they want.

"For a while," I said, "I was sitting where I could see their faces and there was absolutely no change in their expressions."

"Not at all."

"They were listening and looking but there was no change at all. Just a blank expression."

"Yeah. Another thing, I received no sounding voice, nothing to bounce off of, so it was difficult. The other night, you know, you heard me when I spoke to the literary group and it was a different story."

"Yes it was."

"My talks usually come off very well. And the same thing at Mancos that time."

"Right. You get very good response with audiences like the literary group or chamber of commerce members. You mentioned you probably have a thousand books about Indians."

"Yes."

"Some of them written by Indians."

"Yes, I am going to make a list for them. They are having a difficult time and I know the books and they might have a hard time finding them.

"One thing I have found out is that ninety percent of the people in book stores don't know anything about books. There is usually one person in a book store who knows something about them. Lots of times you will go into a book store and ask for a book that you know is available, and they will say, 'I never heard of the book,' 'It's not available,' 'We haven't got it,' 'We don't get it,' or something. This happens a great many times and they may have it in the shelves.

"Actually, I think what I will do is go out to one of the book shops and pick up ten or a dozen of these books, box them up and send them to them. You see, these people have got to find something to identify with. They have lost their roots. They have lost their roots in the world they come from, you know."

"It's a very sad thing, isn't it?"

"It's *a very sad thing*. You bet it is. And yet they have a great deal to contribute. The Indians all the way through their culture have been very intelligent. Given an intelligence test, the Indians usually come off very well. Indians have shown many, many times that given a chance to adapt they can adapt and they are very quick to apply what they know to a situation. But they have to have something to feed on.

"Today I was trying to get them to have the feeling that other Indians had achieved and that they also could achieve if they would. And if I didn't do anything but that I would have given them something.

"But these books I am talking about, some of them tell Indian stories, of Indian background, the stories their grandmother might have told them. Some of them are personal experiences of Indians written by themselves or as told to somebody. It is nice to know they have a literature, that they have a background.

"One reason I mentioned a thousand books is because I wanted to impress on them the knowledge that someone had thought enough of the Indian to write about him. Now I am thoroughly familiar with that literature and you are to a great extent. You feel that you know this is true, but they don't know it is true. They feel like they are very much a minority, very much a second rate people."

"I recall one of the teachers at their school asked you if you could give them the names of some good books written by Indians," I said. "They are the instructors of this class and they should know this, shouldn't they?"

"They should, yes they should. They should know that and they don't. You see another thing about it is their culture has been kind of put down. Now a lot of the Indian schools, while they did it with the best of motives, were very bad about making the Indians always speak English, never their own Indian tongue. And, also, to learn strictly what was being taught in the schools. They were trying to take them away from the old culture entirely. This is a mistake. They should let them have their own culture, let them keep on speaking in their own Indian tongue but also learn English. Because we need all this rich background ourselves, the country needs it.

"One of the strengths of America is the fact that we have drawn people from all over the world," L'Amour continued. "All their cultures have contributed to our culture.

"You see for many, many years the Indian was relatively isolated so he didn't advance very much. He stayed for several hundred years in a hunting, food-gathering sort of culture. Whereas in Europe and Asia, because they were tied together and because there were good seaports over there and everything, there was a lot of moving back and forth, a lot of invasions from other areas, people coming in from out of the country, razing, terrorizing and murdering, but bringing in new ideas and staying there, you see.

"So Europe got a chance to develop, China did also for the same reason. Any country," L'Amour continued as he reached for the thermos of coffee, "where there had been a big interplay among people had lots of new ideas, lots of new ways of doing things.

"Here in this country it was relatively static for a long time, so they had no chance to develop. There was no need to develop beyond where they were. No one was coming along and saying, 'Well, we can do this. This can be done in such and such a way.'

"For example, they used the travois, two poles behind the pony. First it was out behind the dog to carry their equipment on, then they found out about the wheel which changed everything for them. They found out many other things, about the use of metals, but they had barely begun to work with copper. You have to have this interchange between people before you get any intellectual development.

"That is why this country has achieved so much so fast. Because each person has brought in his own background, his own knowledge. The Scandinavians, the English, the French, the Spanish — all of them have come here you know. They have all mingled together and each one had a certain expertise in one way or another. All this put together has enabled us to move ahead at a very rapid pace."

"I am just thinking of the different eating places you have

here in Los Angeles," I said. "You have the Chinese, Japanese, you have the Greek, the Jewish – you have them all, but do you have any Indian restaurant?"

"There is one I know of in Pasadena."

"I mean native Indian."

"No, not native Indian. No there is not. I was thinking of India."

"This is one way traditions are handed down, isn't it?

"Yes. Yes it is."

"So for the native Indian there is no place where one can eat their food."

"That's true, that's true," L'Amour confirmed. "No there isn't. Yet we all have recipes that come from them. We got hominy from them, for example, and any number of other. They gave corn to the world, several varieties of squash, several varieties of melon, beans and peas and a lot of plants that weren't known to the old world. You got both the tomato and potato from our country.

"The Indian populations from South America, Central America and North America did an enormous job of domesticating plants — cotton and cacao,[1] and all kinds of others. You can't begin to name them all."

"Margaret and I were in a book store in Westwood a couple of days ago. She reached up and pulled a book entitled, Zane Grey's Recipes off the shelf." I chuckled.

"Oh, yeah."

"I really didn't look at it close enough, but it's very interesting, isn't it? I think they are capitalizing on his name."

"I think so too." Louis responded.

"Someone is."

"Yeah. I don't know of any recipes he had," Louis added.

"I have thought some about appending one in some of my stories once in a while because I get inquires from people about

---

[1] Seed or bean of an evergreen tree. A small tropical American evergreen tree, cultivated for seeds, the source of cocoa, chocolate, etc.

things mentioned in my stories. One thing I have mentioned in several of my stories that I have never seen anywhere else is corn flour. Corn flour was a substance people used to carry when they were traveling, an emergency food."

"Is it different from corn meal?"

"It is similar to corn meal but they would add a little more to it. Sometimes they would mix in a little bit of brown sugar, sometimes some other substance, often a bit of cinnamon or something. They would carry a sack of this with them and would mix it with a little water. It made a very good emergency food. A lot of people when they were traveling would take a sack of this, carry it across the country and never stop to eat anything else. Take a swallow of this in his mouth, followed by a swallow of water, roll it around in his mouth and swallow it, you know.

"It was a very good food before they had pemmican. Pemmican was something else the Indians gave us. It was one of the most remarkable and I think the best easily portable food there is. The Indians were very knowledgeable about food but they didn't take much time preparing it as a rule.

"Pemmican was made by taking buffalo meat, or venison or any kind of meat, and pounding it until it was all flat and flaky. Then they would pour over that a thin film of melted grease from the buffalo or whatever animal they happened to be using. Then, depending on the Indian or what they had available, they would crush into it some wild strawberries, wild raspberries or other wild fruit. Then they would put over this another layer of meat, another layer of grease, another layer of fruit and more layers of each.

"This would be compressed into a real hard block. You could take a corner of that about as big as a quarter and chew it. It was almost as good as a meal. A man could keep going on this for a long time. After the white man discovered it, they began taking it on polar expeditions and they began making it commercially."

"I will bet, Louis, there were a lot of days in the past when you would have liked to have had something like that."

"Oh, boy, I sure would of," Louis chuckled. "Many, many, times. I would sure have loved it, but I had nothing of the kind."

CHAPTER 13

CONSIDERING THE CRITIC

In 1978, after spending twenty-one years in Jamestown, North Dakota, I was ready to sell our drug store and retire. By this time Meredith and Allan were off on their own, so Margaret and I moved to Greer, South Carolina and built a house in the country on property that had been part of my grandfather's farm. Although we were now located in the foothills of the Blue Ridge Mountains, we named our place Dakota Ranch, bringing a flavor of the west back with us.

On the twelfth day of June, Margaret and I drove to Chattanooga, Tennessee to meet L'Amour's flight from Fort Lauderdale. True to form, Louis was one of the first to disembark. As I drove to our hotel I asked about his meeting in Florida. He told us he had made a speech to members at the Select Magazine Convention in Boca Raton, Florida. Select Magazine is a nationwide distributor of magazines and paperback books.

Once L'Amour told me, "Writing a book is the first step. Getting it published is the second. Selling it is the third." Since then I have thought a lot about the last sentence, "Selling it is the third."

Louis worked hard and was good at selling his product. I was with him on occasions when he was interviewed on television, radio, or by newspaper reporters and when he spoke with his readers at autographing sessions.

We checked in at The Read House, "One of the South's Great Landmark Hotels," where Louis reviewed his research plans for the next two days. He wanted to revisit Shooting Creek, Crab Orchard Mountains and Grassy Cove, then see an old stone fort. He decided to go to the Shooting Creek area and North Carolina the first day. (See map on page 128.)

The next morning we had just been seated at the Read House Restaurant, hungry and ready for breakfast. L'Amour was describing his meeting in Boca Raton. The group consisted mostly of district managers from Little Rock and across the United States and Canada.

"What was the attendance at this meeting?" I asked.

"I don't know," Louis answered. "The actual members were about eighty-three. Each of these represent sales of many thousands of books, you see. Not each of 'em but most of 'em did. Then of course some of them had their wives along and there were other people there. For instance, there were quite a few of the SM Magazine people who weren't really connected with the book business. They wanted to know what was going on."

"Were these employees of Select Magazine?"

"There were a couple of other publishers there who wanted to keep track of what is going on, but the actual membership of those who were supposed to be there was eighty-three."

"Then they are out in the field aren't they?" I asked. "They are the ones who head the districts of Select Magazine."

"Some of the other fellows were there, too. For example, there were distributors down there with whom Select works, but they also distribute other books. A number of those were there. There was quite a gathering in all.

"Really, it was my meeting. I am not exaggerating. As a matter of fact, they put out these western hats with 'SM Loves Louis' on the band."

"Where can we order them?"

"I guess the only place you can get them is Select Magazine."

"Do you know their address?" I asked.

"Off hand I don't but I can get it for you. I will try and get some for you."

"That would be a gem in my collection."

"It would be nice to wear one when you give your talks on Louis in South Carolina," Margaret added.

"You see, each of these eighty-three people was given a hat. I suppose they got a bargain deal on the hats and just before I got up to speak they all put on the hats. It was fun."

Looking at the menu, Louis said, "Well, well, well, let's see."

"We could go over there and get some things," Margaret said. "Is that a buffet?"

"They have a whole lot of things on ice. It's pretty classy here. Quite like the Strater in Durango, Colorado."

"Do they have sausage or bacon over there?" Louis asked.

"I suppose," Margaret commented. "I haven't seen it all but the waitress will probably tell us. There is some cereal and some fruit."

The waitress came to our table and, in answer to our question, listed a number of items on the buffet. Margaret asked the price. It was $2.50. She said, "I guess I will order from the menu."

"I want some meat," Louis said. "Everything looks very good, but I like to order from the menu." The waitress left and we visited while examining the menu.

"I may have to get maps tonight because that company may not open until 9 or 9:30 tomorrow."

"Maybe we can find out at the desk," I suggested. "I want to get another copy of <u>Fair Blows the Wind</u>.

"Louis, have you seen this <u>Roundup</u>?" I asked, indicating a copy I had put on our table. "In it there is a letter to the editor from me responding to a reviewer of your books."

"No, I have the <u>Roundups</u> but I haven't read them yet. I get behind with some of those things."

"The reviewer identified your book as, "<u>Where the Tall Grass Grows</u> when it should have been <u>Where the Long Grass Blows</u>."

"That's right."

"It wasn't complimentary. He writes westerns himself and I think his judgment of others might be distorted. In response to his review I wrote the editor and my letter was published. Do you want to read it?"

"Yeah, I would like to very much. I belong to this organization but they don't like me very much because my sales are so huge. Will Henry who is perhaps the best of the . . . "

The waitress returned to take our order.

"Margaret?" Louis asked.

"You go ahead, I haven't quite decided."

"I'll have a large glass of orange juice, a side of sausage and the sweetest sweet roll you have," Louis ordered with a big smile.

"How many checks?" the waitress asked.

"One check," said Louis. "I'll put it on the bill."

"Before you start that Louis," I said when L'Amour turned back to the magazine, "he also used <u>The Burning Land</u> referring to another one of your books. Should have been <u>The Burning Hills</u>. Now you can understand the purpose of my letter."

"Yeah. The writer must be a little jealous. There is no reason for all this. There is room for all of us, you know. My sales come to half of all the westerns sold in all the world, and the rest of these guys sold the other half."

"That's a little something to be jealous about," said Margaret.

"Yeah," Louis agreed. "Will Henry, however, who is perhaps the best of the crowd, has written two of the finest complimentary letters that I have ever had from anybody. Just marvelous. I'll show them to you sometime."

"Harold Keith, in his three part article, [1] did a terrific job I thought." I added.

"Yes it was very good."

"In the last part of the series he used a quote from you telling 'Why you write about the West.' I've wanted to ask you if this is an accurate quote."

"Yes, I think it is. As I remember he quoted me very accurately. He was the sports editor at the University of Oklahoma for a long time."

"So," I said. "I think I will continue to use that in my talks."

"Yeah, go ahead," Louis said.

"It gives such a good picture of why you write about the west."

"Yeah, he does a good job. He is a good writer," Louis added, turning to read the letter in the Roundup.

"Very nice," he commented when he had finished.

"I couldn't let that ride."

"No. You certainly answered it very well too."

"This wasn't the end of it. In my letter I didn't mention a thing about what I thought about your books, did I?"

"No." Louis said.

I handed over the reviewer's response to my letter and L'Amour read it.

"You see what he did," I explained. "He agreed with my unfavorable opinion about your book when I didn't even state an opinion. This must be what you go through many times."

"Well," Louis said in his kind way, "for example, you know,

---

[1] In The Roundup, December 1975 and January and February of 1976.

a review came out – it is difficult in a sense – I understand the reviewer's position. They are reviewing one book and don't have the sense of all I have done.

"A reviewer of <u>Fair Blows The Wind</u> said it was apparent that I was trying to change my image by writing this type of book and made some comment about westerns. It doesn't make any difference to me. I am teaching the young people to read valiantly and not trying to change my image. You see had he known about the three families[2] . . . . "

"There would have been no question."

"There would be no question. But he didn't know about them."

[2] Sackett, Chantry and Talon.

CHAPTER 14

CHASING HISTORY IN GRASSY COVE, TENNESSEE

Forty miles north of Chattanooga Louis looked into the back seat at Margaret. With a twinkle in his eye he asked, "Isn't it about time for us to stop for coffee and doughnuts?"

"Aha. It's ten o'clock," she said. "Time for North Dakotans to have morning coffee and homemade doughnuts! But I doubt if we will find any here."

Lo and behold, in the next town, Pikeville, we found just that. Sitting in a sunny booth by the window in a pleasant cafe we marveled at our good fortune – homemade doughnuts.[1]

The air was crystal clear on this June day in 1978. After thirty years L'Amour was returning to a beautiful five-mile-long valley in the heartland of Eastern Tennessee. As we drove slowly along the peaceful road that parted the lush green sheltered hollow, I thought how appropriate was its name — Grassy Cove.

On both sides the fertile land was a pattern of crops and pastures. To our right cattle were grazing. All this was circled by a range of low mountains.

After driving the full length of the cove, Louis asked me to turn the car around. He wanted to verify the mileage from one end of the cove to the other. I set the trip mileage on zero.

---

[1] Recipe on page 127.

Our stop at the first of two country stores was brief. We were told Emily Kemmer was very knowledgeable about this area. She lived across the road from the second store, so we went there to contact her and she walked over to join us in front of the store. Mrs. Kemmer was an attractive woman who came to Grassy Cove several years earlier as a county home economist.

After introductions Margaret told Mrs. Kemmer, "I am a native of North Dakota, L'Amour's home state."

"Los Angeles is now my home," L'Amour told her. "I came from North Dakota originally and Margaret and Reese used to live there. They now live in Greer, South Carolina."

He told her he was researching another book and Grassy Cove was one of the places he planned to use in his story.

"This is fiction you are writing, isn't it?" asked Mrs. Kemmer.

"Uh huh. It is all based on history. You see, I take a couple of fictitious characters and put them in actual historical situations. One thing I'm interested in is finding out if there are any relics around here – arrowheads or things of that nature."

"Well, I don't know very much about arrowheads. There are always, you know, some people looking for those things. We know the Indians were here."

We entered the store and, as I listened to their conversation, I looked around. Old country stores had fascinated my family for a long time. In fact, I got my name from a man who ran an old-timey one.

My grandfather traded at Mr. Reese's country store, a few miles from where they lived in upstate South Carolina. Many times he took my dad, who was a young lad, with him on these trips. Mr. Reese treated my dad like royalty.

"Good morning, Allan," he greeted him. "Come right in. Sit here on this stool in front of the fireplace."

Mr. Reese then walked over to the shelf where he kept candy

in small paper boxes. He always gave young Allan one and sometimes two pieces.

Later, to honor Mr. Reese, my dad changed his name from
Allan Jerry to Allan Reese, becoming Allan Reese Hawkins.
I am his namesake.

"Come over here," Mrs. Kemmer said to Louis. "I will show
you this little book about Grassy Cove. It was out of print until this
past year and this friend has republished it. It's an early history of
the Cove telling about the people who were here, where they came
from and this sort of thing. Here's the little book."

"Can I get it in Crossville?" Louis asked.

"Yes. I was going to give you the name of the man who re-
printed this. Would you like to have it?"

"Yes, I would like that."

"Here is something else you might be interested in," she said
to L'Amour.

Louis looked at the cover of the publication. "Oh, yes. I would
like that!"

"I think when you get the one about Grassy Cove you can
get this from the same place."

I stepped over to look at the publications. The first was entitled, Grassy Cove and the second, Tales of the Civil War Era.

"We have so many people who come here who are interested
in this area from a geographical standpoint," Mrs. Kemmer told
us. "You see, the only outlet for the surface water goes underground
into this cave up here. We have people who come from everywhere to go and see that."

"I want to see that too," Louis said. "Both of these books are
very important to me."

Mrs. Kemmer showed L'Amour pictures from another publication.

"This is where the water goes in."

"I see."

"All the water that falls in this valley is drained underground through this cave at the base of the mountain." Another picture showed where it came out on the other side of the mountain, reappearing as a river. "One man has done an awful lot of study on that."

Louis said, "I want to get a copy of this too if. . . ."

"What is the name of it?" I asked.

"That's a government publication," Mrs. Kemmer said.

"Is it a monthly publication?"

"Yes. This is cave information, etc."

Louis asked if there were any other caves in the cove.

"Yes. Yes, there are a number of caves. There is one called the Saltpeter Cave."

"Yeah?" from Louis.

"And that's where they found the saltpeter for the gunpowder," Mrs. Kemmer continued.

"Perfect! I can use that," Louis said emphatically.

"Old hoppers were in that cave," Mrs. Kemmer added, "but they have been destroyed. People go in that cave just all the time and they tell me there are lots of rooms and lots of places that can be explored. I have been in it one time. I am not a caver myself."

"Where is this cave?" I asked.

"Well, it is in this valley. Of course if you are interested in going, I will give you specific directions. It's about a mile and a half from here."

I asked Louis if he was interested in seeing it.

"Yes, I am."

"Mrs. Kemmer," I said, "This is exactly what Louis is looking for."

"Louis will have his fictional characters come into the cove here and they will find this cave," Margaret added.

He said he would have the Sacketts run out of gunpowder and make their own from the saltpeter. "They were making their own gunpowder anyway. Are there any lead mines around here?"

"No."

"There used to be some over east of here," Louis said. "I know a couple of places where they used to get some. The Indians used to have one place over there that nobody ever found."

"Let's see, another book you should read is <u>Cumberland County The First 100 Years</u>. Have you seen that?"

"Yes, I have. I have that. It's a good book – this is excellent!"

"I'll tell you who to look for to get these books. He's Donald Brookhart.[2] He has a place in Crossville."

At our stop at the first Kemmer store, John Kemmer had mentioned a L'Amour fan who had a store and sold L'Amour's books. We asked her who this might be.

"Oh! I'll bet that's Hill's Department Store in Crossville." She told us Les Hill sold western books and gave us directions to his place. Les was her cousin. "He's a good advertiser for your books," she added. "Look for Hill's Department Store. You can't miss it."

We could not have found a more gracious, helpful and knowledgeable person than Mrs. Kemmer. She walked out of the store with us. Louis, Margaret and I were ready to hike to the cave where the water left the valley. Before giving us the directions she mentioned there were rattlesnakes in the area.

"Well, we won't go there," said Louis without hesitation.

If it weren't for those snakes we would have seen the saltpeter cave and where the water disappeared.

I recalled a passage in L'Amour's <u>To the Far Blue Mountains</u> where Barnabas Sackett was wondering why things sometime happen the way they do. The one day we showed up unan-

---

[2] The <u>News Sentinel</u> identified G. Donald Brookhart as Cumberland County Historian.

nounced at Grassy Cove Mrs. Kemmer was there.

Leaving this cozy cove for the return drive to Crossville, I looked at the mileage. Almost exactly five miles.

"My personal feeling is," Louis said, "this valley can be proud of the Kemmers. Nice intelligent people and they keep their places beautiful."

"Would be a nice place to live," Margaret added.

"So many times you come into a valley like this and everything is so rundown," Louis commented. "I had forgotten that Saltpeter Cave was in here, and that makes it perfect, you know. The people on the frontier in the very early days had to make their own gunpowder often as not. The Indians did too."

CHAPTER 15

MEETING A READER AT THE B & W CAFE

"Look!" Margaret announced. "There's a Hill's Department Store sign on top of that building. Reese, find a parking place."

Louis L'Amour, Margaret and I arrived in Crossville, Tennessee a little before noon on this June day in 1978 and were driving slowly along its main street.

"Maybe we should not disturb him," said L'Amour. There were certain circumstances when he hesitated to intrude on the privacy of others. This was one of them.

I told Louis if he had been in Jamestown and passed our store knowing I was a fan of his and didn't stop in, it would have been a terrible disappointment.

Margaret and I entered the store and, walking to the rear, asked an employee if Les Hill was in.

"No, he isn't," she replied. "May I help you?"

I told her we understood Mr. Hill was a fan of Louis L'Amour and Mr. L'Amour was out front in our car.

"We would like to have Les join us for lunch," I said.

"Just a minute," she said. Her hand shook slightly as she punched in a phone number. I felt she literally wanted to hold on to us to keep us there.

She repeated our invitation to Mrs. Hill. Moments later Les Hill was on the phone. After a brief interchange, she told us Mr. Hill would meet us at the B and W Cafe.

We were only a short distance from the cafe and arrived before Mr. Hill. Louis chose a table with his back to the wall and a view of the entire dining area. When possible he liked to do this. It enabled him to absorb the atmosphere of the place, the activity around him. This custom was typical of the old west. Louis must have developed this practice during his younger days.

We had just settled at our table when Les Hill walked in the front door and headed straight for us.

"Welcome to Tennessee, Mr. L'Amour!" Both his face and voice reflected pleasure as he greeted us. When he seated himself at our square table, I thought of the hundreds of thousands of fans who would have come from all over – just to be sitting at the same table in the B and W Cafe with Louis L'Amour.

"What new books do you have out?" was Les's first question.

"I have two, <u>Mountain Valley War</u> and <u>Fair Blows the Wind</u> in hard-cover. <u>Fair Blows the Wind</u> will be out in paperback around August."

Margaret asked Les if he had any of Louis' hard-covers.

"No, I haven't. Haven't seen 'em."

"You've got a treat coming," she said.

"What might interest you some is I am going to move the Sacketts into Grassy Cove . . ." L'Amour commented.

"O-o-oh!" Les interrupted. "My! Really? Way back, that's where my mother and grandfather lived!"

"I don't know if you have read <u>Sackett's Land</u>," L'Amour continued.

"Oh yeah. I have."

"Well, in <u>To The Far Blue Mountains</u> I moved the Sacketts from over in the Blue Ridge Mountains to Shooting Creek where they settled and raised their family. The old man, Barnabas, got killed up in the mountains near Crab Orchard when they were scouting for a new home. A couple of his boys are going to settle in Grassy Cove. I was there about thirty years ago – never forgot the place."

Les was exuberant. "It's a beautiful place all right."

"Lovely," added Louis.

"I've read your stories and get a lot out of them. I've had a lot of pleasure reading them. You know, I just get lost in them, I don't want nobody around, I just get with it. I have spent a lot of time in the west and I love it. I try to look up the places where all these things happen. You know, if you can't go out there, your books are the nearest to it."

Les not only appreciated Louis' stories, he could tell a good one himself. He told us about his trip to hunt elk in Wyoming.

"I picked up a couple of fellows at the airport in Denver. We went up to Granby, spent the night, and the next morning we went up this beautiful valley. We stopped at Willow Creek, coming in from the south end of it. We got up early, hadn't had breakfast. We stopped in this little town.

"Just walked inside," Les continued, "and here was this old boy, drunk, sitting on a stool. It was 8:30 or 9:00 in the morning."

"Yeah," Louis chuckled.

"He had a bunch of boys around him. We got to shooting the bull with him and he just wouldn't let us go. We were huntin' breakfast, you know, we were in a restaurant. Out there everything has a bar in it."

"Sure," said Louis.

"We got to talking with him and he asked us where we were going."

" 'We're going elk hunting', was our answer."

"'Where?' he asked.

"'Wyoming,' I told him.

"He said, 'Hell, you don't have to go to Wyoming. You can go right here. I was up on the range all summer and I saw elk all over the place. I can get you all you want.' We said, 'Red, we don't have permission to hunt here in Colorado.' He said, 'that don't make no difference.' "

Another chuckle from L'Amour.

"So he asked, 'Where are you from?'

"We said Tennessee. He said 'So am I.'

"How long have you been out here?" I asked.

"He said, 'Ever since I was 16,' said he was from Sevierville. That's in Eastern Tennessee in the mountains you know."

"Yeah, I know," Louis said.

"I asked him how come you came out here so young," Les continued, "and he said, 'My daddy killed my granddaddy when I was 16 years old and I figured it was time for Red to leave home.'"

From Louis, another subdued laugh.

"He said he had been up in the mountains all summer," Les continued. "And had just come back in the night before and brought the herd in. He said the old lady, the rancher's wife, sat him down to a cheeseburger and a pack of potato chips. He just told her to go to Hell. He thought he ought to have the biggest steak in the world, you know. He told her if that was all she thought of him, he was going to quit. So he turned his time in.

"He must have had twelve to fourteen hundred dollars in his pocket. Every time he put his hand in his pocket it would all fall out on the floor. Just like a shock of hay. He had it all balled up and everything. Man, he was sitting on ready!

"One of my friends was standing up right next to him," Les said. "Red kept talking and he asked my friend, he said, 'big boy, have a drink.' My friend said, 'Naw, it's too early for me, Red.'

And he punched my friend in his chest again and said, 'Big boy you had better have that drink!' My friend said, 'You know Red, I have been thinking about this and I believe I will.' "

"Some of these people like to have you drink with them," Louis said, "and think you are insulting them if you don't."

"Yeah," Les agreed. "I just eased around, had my breakfast and left. I let the rest of the boys do the talking."

This story was typical of many L'Amour listened to during his early years when he moved from job to job and town to town.

"I don't drink but I've spent a lot of time in bars," said Louis. "That's when you hear a lot of stories from old-timers. If you take time to listen to them, you will learn something." One time Louis had to fight to defend himself when he turned down a fellow's offer to have a drink.

Our conversation returned to the present. Les asked L'Amour where Shalako, a town Louis planned to build, would be located. It was to be a composite replica of a small western town that existed during the period Louis writes about.

"This will be located eleven miles west of Durango," Louis explained. "Look on the map and find Hesperus. Our town will be one mile north of Hesperus where we own the post office building, the trading post and the motel. The La Plata river runs right through our property, comes right down from the La Plata Mountains. We have 2000 acres there."

We told Les about meeting John Kemmer and his son at our first stop in Grassy Cove. Les told us both of them are educated, as he was. All have college degrees. The son, also named John Kemmer was about fifty-eight years old.

"That's a pretty little valley," Louis said, speaking of Grassy Cove.

"It's the nicest in the spring of the year," said Les, "when the grass is just coming up and the cattle are belly deep in that grass."

"I just fell in love with it," said Louis. "I came through here about thirty years ago, fell in love with it and have never forgotten it. I was thinking of moving the Sacketts in there and had to come back and take another look. What pleased me so much is it is just as I remembered it."

"I am fifty-five years old," Les said, "and I can remember how it was when I was a little kid. Every Sunday we went down there, you know. My mother was born and raised there."

Margaret asked Les about the pictures that were on the wall in the store. They were of Les' grandparents. He said the old store was across the creek and is still standing. Old patent medicines fifty years old, still with labels on them, were on display. Louis mentioned John Kemmer Jr. told us arrowheads were sometimes found in the valley.

"I just don't think you are writing enough damn books, Louis." Les said.

"Well, I am trying to do better."

"You see, I am second or third time around on most of them. I just date them when I have read them last. Let's see, I've got sixty-five at home and five of 'em loaned out."

"Have to check them out I guess," said Margaret.

"Well, I have a list of those I give them to. They have my name on them and, dog gone right, if they don't return them they don't get any more of them."

"Does Louis have quite a few fans here?" asked Margaret.

"Very much so, very much so."

"I'll say," he said, looking at Louis, "you are the hottest thing going. You are! You know it yourself, no question about it."

"Thank you," L'Amour responded, "Yes, well, seventy-seven million was the last figure I had." Louis failed to add that at this time his sales were three times that of Zane Grey. L'Amour had become one of three best-selling authors of all time.

"How did you get started reading L'Amour's books?" Margaret asked Les.

"I read everything Zane Grey ever wrote, I guess. When my grandparents died, they had some Zane Grey books in their library and my mother got them, so they were around the house. I read all of them. Some of them just fell apart. Then I got to reading some Luke Short stuff, the *Saturday Evening Post*, the continued stories you know.

"I have always liked the West," Les continued. "I never had a chance to go there, to the true West, until '52. Then I saw it, the Yellowstone area and Wyoming. I think the Tetons are the most beautiful area you can be in."

"Spectacular," L'Amour interjected.

"To me that Snake River overlook is the best view I have seen anywhere. There is some beautiful country up in Montana."

"Do you remember when you first read a L'Amour book?" I asked Les.

"Somebody mentioned it to me, wanted to know if I'd read any of them. I said no, I've never read them. This was in the late 60's. I don't know which one I read first."

"I wish I could remember which one I read first," I added. "I will never forget the occasion. After reading the first, I moved through the others real fast."

"It was <u>The Broken Gun</u>," Les recalled. "I have read all of them at least twice, except <u>Bourdon Chantry,</u> or something like that."

Louis helped him out. "<u>Borden Chantry</u>. I read the Zane Grey books too when I was a kid."

"He had a knack of painting a pretty good picture too," Les said. "When the sun went down you could see it."

"Yeah, that's right," Louis agreed. "I try to put the reader into the story, so he is right there and can see and hear everything that is going on."

"Zane Grey was slow in getting you into the story. The thing you've got that Zane Grey didn't have, you get down to the action. You get the reader into the story right away."

I told Les we were at Shooting Creek yesterday, then saw the area where Barnabas was killed.

"You did? He was that old boy, the first of the Sacketts, wasn't he? From England?"

"Yeah," Louis answered. "He is the original ancestor of that crowd. He was in <u>Sackett's Land</u> and <u>To the Far Blue Mountains</u>. They make their final settlement in Shooting Creek over here."

"It's east of Chattanooga, about one hundred miles," Margaret added.

"It is when you are going toward Franklin,"[1] said Louis. "The highway skirts it now. You would like it, you might like to go down through there. The Sacketts keep moving west generation by generation. They are going into Grassy Cove next."

"What are you going to name it, do you know?" Les asked.

"No. I don't yet."

"When we were leaving Grassy Cove a little while ago," Margaret said, "we all wondered why the Sacketts would want to leave it and go west. It was so pretty there."

"It got too slow down there." Les had figured it out.

"Yes," Louis added. "They had to go west."

"They were men of action," Les said.

---

[1] Franklin is in the western North Carolina mountains, south of the Great Smoky Mountains National Park.

CHAPTER 16

SCALPING BY SIOUX —
THEN SIGNING FOR PEACE

"If you come to Colorado again, come in August and look me up," Louis said to Les Hill. "I am always there in August. I have a condominium at Tamarron right outside of Durango."

"These fellows you loan your books to aren't going to believe it when you tell them you had lunch with Louis L'Amour today and were invited to his place in Colorado," said Margaret.

"There's one woman," Les said, "I'll tell you she's an old lady. Now she gets these old books that have 25 cents on them. She just goes around to flea markets and buys them for a dime apiece. She says she likes them better than these old modern-day westerns – all but you, Louis. She swears by you. She does! She says that Louis L'Amour is the best one yet. Now that includes Zane Grey. She will come in the store and we will talk a long time.

"She took a couple of trips out west, not able monetarily to take a lot of trips, but when she does she sees a lot of places. Purgatory and all that, you know. There are two or three places she wants to go and writes them down. She wants me to look them up the next time I go out there to see what they look like."

"Yeah," Louis nodded his head.

"I'd like you to autograph one of your books for her," Les

said.

"I'll be glad to," Louis responded.

"She won't be worth a tinker's damn for a month after she gets your autographed book!" Les exclaimed.

"Is Purgatory near Durango?" Margaret asked L'Amour.

"Yes, it is. I have one old gentleman out there, he is ninety-three years old now, and his son declares I have kept him alive the last twelve years . . . "

Margaret laughed.

". . . because he reads one of my books," Louis continued, "then gets in his camper and goes out there."

"Yeah, got to look it over," Les put in. "Sure, you know this is good, gets in your blood. My wife thinks I am a nut but I love the West, can't help it."

"Me, too," Louis agreed.

Then the waitress returned and suggested pie for dessert. We were all silent for a moment or two as she listed several choices: apple, chess, strawberry, cherry and walnut.[1]

Margaret, Les and I made choices, but Louis told the waitress, "You pick me out a piece and I will just take your selection."

"Want a walnut?" she asked.

"Whatever you say," Louis responded with a big smile.

"Change mine to walnut," said Margaret.

"Mine too," I added.

"Les?" Margaret asked.

"Well, ok, let's make it unanimous."

"I have a lot of friends among the Indians out there," L'Amour said, returning to the discussion of the West. "Early last year they had a peace treaty signing, Comanches and Utes. They fought for 250 years and decided to sign a peace treaty."

"Well I'll be dogged," said Les.

---

[1] The recipe for walnut pie is at the end of this chapter.

"They asked me to come and be the official historian."

"That's great."

"They danced for four days and four nights, really a lot of fun."

Les asked if they had any "fire water" with them.

"No, not in this place they wouldn't," Louis said. "This was a semi-religious ceremony. Outside they did, but not around there. The Comanches danced what was called The Black Knife Dance. The Comanche's Black Man Society was never defeated in battle by anybody, white man or Indian.

"This was supposed to be a victory dance. Well, the victory dance for the Indian means a scalp dance. They warned everybody beforehand. They had a towel. Had to keep it tied up or hold it in their arms. Dogs were strictly taboo. If one came out during this dance they would kill it. Before the dance starts a guy goes all around the area dancing with bow and arrow in his hands hunting for dogs."

"Was the Comanche a Plains Indian?" Les asked L'Amour.

"Yes. You see the Ute used to come down out of the mountains, Ute is a mountain Indian, you know, to hunt buffalo. They would run into the Comanche and fights resulted. The Comanche used to go back up in the mountains and canyons in hot weather. They would run into the Utes and fights took place."

"Didn't they like to fight, though?" Les asked. "They weren't mad at each other, they just liked to fight."

"They liked to fight of course. A man wasn't a man until he had taken a scalp. He couldn't speak in their council, he couldn't get a girl, he couldn't do anything."

"You know," Les said, "I think I would like to read about this rather than to have been there."

"Kind of rough – kind of rough," Louis softly answered.

"Course a lot of books I read have to do with the northern

Sioux," Les said. "They were pretty wild out there, weren't they?"

"They killed my great-grandfather."

"Really?"

"Reese has been out there where he was killed," Louis said.

"Where was that?" asked Les.

"North Dakota."

"I have an enlarged picture of the marker showing the location where he was killed," I added. "The marker reads, 'Lt. Ambrose Freeman was shot by the Sioux and buried here in 1863.' This was about ten miles north of Tappen, North Dakota. I've walked over the area. It's near where the Battle of Big Mound took place."[2]

"Was he in the Cavalry?" Les asked.

"My great-grandfather was in command of a group called the Northern Rangers. He was born in Virginia and when the Civil War came on he didn't believe in the cause of the South. He didn't want to fight against them, so he got transferred out there to fight the Indians.

"They had him organize the Northern Rangers. Their job was to protect the settlements while the army was gone. Everything was rather quiet. All of a sudden Little Crow raised up overnight and killed between 800 and 1000 people, depending on whose figures you take.

"My great-grandfather with seventy-five Rangers had to try to do something with 3000 Indians. Then they sent Sibley up there with a command. They chased the Indians out across the Dakota plains. My great-grandfather would have been about fifty years old when he was scalped. My grandfather was with the same outfit.

Les brought up the subject of the white man-Indian conflict.

L'Amour's thinking was: "There were two sides to the question. I don't know that anyone was to blame. It was the way it happened, that's all. Part of it was how the Indian society was organized.

---

[2] Edna LaMoore Waldo, Louis' sister, wrote about this in a book entitled, <u>Yet She Follows</u>.

"In the first place the old Indians began to see it was time to make peace, they couldn't buck the white man. As I had an Indian say in one of my stories, 'We killed them and killed them and they still kept coming'.

"There was one little ranch out in western Nebraska where the people were killed five different times. Five different families were wiped out. When one was killed another would move in and start all over again. The Indians finally gave up on them.

"But anyway, the old Indians had stolen their horses, they had their wives, they could speak in council. They were big men in the tribe. They had their status so they were ready to settle down and call it quits. What was the young man going to do who wanted all that?"

"He hadn't done all this," Les commented.

"That's right," Louis said.

"The older Indians had realized their dreams. They had done all these things and signed peace treaties. The young Indians had yet to reach these goals so they broke the treaties and fought like the older ones did when they were young.

"White men couldn't understand," continued L'Amour. "They thought when you sit down and make peace with the Indians that was it. They couldn't understand why the Indians kept on fighting."

We had finished our lunch. Les Hill picked up the check saying, "In Crossville it's on me."

Then he took us to meet Patricia Kirkeminde, owner of the Purple Bookcase. This bookstore is where we spent the rest of our time while in Crossville.

Activity began when we entered the bookstore. Les used the phone to call county historian, G. Donald Brookhart. While we waited for him to join us, Louis had an opportunity to visit with Patricia. She showed and discussed with him a number of books written about the area.

Soon Mr. Brookhart arrived. He and Louis began a discussion which included the book entitled <u>Cumberland County, First 100 Years</u>. While they were talking Les contacted a speleologist[3] who arrived in a few minutes with charts of Grassy Cove. These were spread on the floor of an adjoining room where this specialist then pointed out and explained locations of some of the many caves to L'Amour. Because of the large number of caverns in this area, it has been described as the "world's largest sinkhole" and was named a National Landmark by the US Department of Interior.[4]

Margaret and I spent the time talking with Les Hill and some L'Amour readers who appeared almost from nowhere. They waited until there was a break to meet Louis and get his autograph.

Usually when L'Amour was researching an area he looked for material of a historical nature written by local people. He then purchased a number of these books (as he did in this case) and had them shipped to his home where they would be read and become part of his extensive library.

After expressing appreciation for all this valuable help, we left to continue our trip back to Chattanooga. We had found Crossville, the "biggest small town in the South," a hospitable oasis in the center of historical Cumberland County.

Mid-afternoon found us driving southwest on highway 70 toward Manchester and the Old Stone Fort. As we moved through the rolling land to our last stop, Louis said, "Very few know about this ancient fort. I would like to see it."

During this relaxing interval our thoughts returned to our visits at the B and W Cafe and the Purple Bookcase.

"Les Hill was certainly a congenial, pleasant guy," Louis said.

"Wasn't he!" I responded.

"I went in there with just the intention of giving the fellow a

---

[3] One who explores and conducts a scientific study of caves.
[4] Article by Bob Fowler, 6/20/98, <u>Crossville Chronicle</u>.

moment of satisfaction because he had read my books and thought it would be kind of fun to go in and shake hands with him. That was all I expected."

"Well, we all had a good time," Margaret responded.

"Very good!" added Louis.

I think it was as exciting a surprise for us, as it was for all of them, because we had not expected this to be such a profitable stop. We had not realized how many knowledgeable and well-informed people would come forward with information.

Unfortunately our arrival at the Old Stone Fort[5] late that afternoon coincided with the museum's closing hour. A sign at the entrance to this National Park headquarters stated that the fort was built by the Phoenicians, the Vikings or the Indians. Being ever proud of her Icelandic ancestry, Margaret, on her own without any scientific research, decided it had to be the Vikings.

John Molberg, a State Forester and college professor in Bottineau, North Dakota, did extensive research on the Turtle Mountains. They lie in the center of the state on the border with Canada. John found physical evidence that the Vikings could have been in that area.[6]

Louis, when questioned about the presence of Vikings in North Dakota, said they certainly could have been there. They were all over, in many places like Heavener, Oklahoma. He went on to say the Phoenicians, who were great seagoing people, were very smart and capable as well. He also thought the Indians could have built it. This is a question which has not yet been answered.

Now the thinking is the Indians built the fort and it was used

---

[5] Old Stone Fort State Archaeological Area is 4.5 mi. n. on U.S. 41 from I-24 exit 114. Part of a 760 acre park in a 2000 year old American Indian ceremonial site. The combination of mounds, walls, cliffs and rivers form a 1.25 mile boundary enclosing 50 acres. A museum displays exhibits relating to the history and legends of the fort and its builders. AAA Kentucky Tennessee Tour Book (valid through November 1998)

[6] Molberg's research began in 1983. He located mooring stones and a stone cave along with a Roman sword. His publication entitled <u>Vikings</u> describes his research in detail.

by them as a ceremonial site. The walls of this ancient ruin have been radiocarbon dated to approximately A.D. 30, A.D. 230, and A.D. 430, so that over a period of four hundred years or so the walls deteriorated and were rebuilt several times.

Though we were able to look only at portions of the walls of the fort and secure material about its history, Louis felt it was a worthwhile stop.

TENNESSEE'S WALNUT PIE

Jamestown's Martha Klingenberg, native of Tennessee

Prepare pie crust in 9 inch pan. Make the filling:

Cream until fluffy:
1/2 cup butter
1 cup sugar

Add: 1 t. vanilla
1/4 t. salt

Add 3 eggs, one at a time, beating after each.

Add 1 1/2 cups walnuts
(raisins and dates may be part of this)

Pour into unbaked crust. Bake at 350 degrees for 40 minutes.

BOTTINEAU NORTH DAKOTA DOUGHNUTS
Sigga Benson, Margaret's mother

3 T. shortening	1 t. baking powder
1 c. sugar	1/2 t. soda
2 eggs, beaten	1/2 t. salt
1 c. buttermilk	3 1/2 - 4 cups flour

Cream shortening and sugar well, add the beaten eggs, liquid, flour and other 3 ingredients. No spices nor vanilla — "the frying gives the flavor," said Sigga. Chill 30 minutes. On a lightly floured surface roll out to 1/2 inch thickness. Cut with a doughnut cutter and move each to a lightly floured board.

Heat 2-3 inches of lard or vegetable shortening to 375 degrees. Fry several at a time (allowing room for expansion) until golden brown edges show. Flip over carefully with a fork, fry on other side. Lift out and place on paper towel.

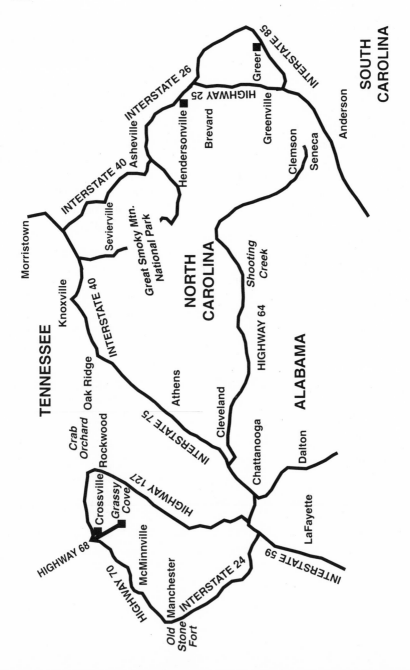

CHAPTER 17

TRAILING THE GILLESPIE RIFLE

"We have just come up South Mills Road," Bert Sitton Jr. told us on a Sunday afternoon, February 3, 1980. "We are standing in a field where the old iron forge originally stood. This field has just been plowed. You will notice those big humps of – looks almost like rocks – but this is iron flag[1] that came out of the old iron forge. Sometimes you will find pieces here that weigh up to fifty or hundred pounds."

A couple of weeks earlier Louis L'Amour had called us to find out if Margaret and I would like to help him locate a Gillespie rifle. He wanted to purchase one. He had information about a Mrs. Patton in Hendersonville, North Carolina, who owned one. On our first trip up the mountains to Hendersonville (about forty-five miles from our home in the Pleasant Hill section north of Greer, South Carolina) we found that Mrs. Patton had given her Gillespie rifle to a museum.

In a casual conversation with Sue Hahn, a member of our Lutheran church, we told her of our project. At the time we did not know her maiden name was Sitton and that she was a descendant of the Sitton family who operated the forge where iron for the Gillespie rifles was made. Within two or three days she had contacted her uncle, Bert Sitton Jr., and arranged for the three of us to

---

[1] The word flag comes from Old Norse or Icelandic *flaga* meaning slab of stone.

meet him and his wife in Hendersonville.

After we finished lunch, Bert Sitton became our tour guide. He was to show us around and introduce us to Bob Gillespie, who still owned one of his family's rifles.

"You notice the South Mills River comes right down beside the forge," Sitton continued. "The power for driving it, that made the big bellows and hammers go, was taken from a mill stream that came off the Old Mill River. Later on there was a saw mill, a grist mill, etc. that also got power from the water of the river here."

I asked Bert how this water power was used in the operation of the forge.

"It lifted these big old hammers and bellows to crunch the iron ore. They had to bust it up into little pieces and then they heated it with coke which they made from chestnut wood cut off of Forge Mountain here. It took weeks to make it – get this iron ore real hot until it melted. Then they would rake off the flag, the pieces of impurities that came off the iron. That's what we are finding here.

"Then they would take the pure iron and make it into what they called *welts*. This was used to make wagon wheels, axes, plows and just about anything the pioneers would use. They used this iron also in the manufacture of the long rifle.

"Sitton came to this location first," Bert continued. After he got his iron works established John Gillespie came here to get the iron to use in making his rifles. His original rifle-making shop was about thirty miles from here. John had three sons who located here — Robert, Matthew, and William. Matthew Gillespie was the one who came down to get the iron and it seems he fell in love with Phillip Sitton's oldest daughter and they were married. Matthew then set his gun shop right here alongside the forge."

"Did one of the Gillespie sons make better rifles than his brothers?" I asked.

"All of them that I have seen were very similar. It seems that there are more Phillip Gillespie rifles in this area than any other. The one you will see later today is one of Phillip's who was the son of Matthew. All together John had five sons. The other two went to Georgia in 1850. All five became rifle makers. Phillip, on the side, had a little distillery up here and made a little brandy. He had a government license."

I wished L'Amour could have been with us as he was when we researched in Grassy Cove, Tennessee. This experience could have been added to the many others he had on location and later wrote about.

Up on a hill was the old Sitton-Gillespie graveyard, still in use at this time. One of the tombstones was made by W. O. Wolfe, the father of the famous Asheville writer Thomas Wolfe[2]. Graves went back to the 1830's. Phillip Sitton was the original iron maker, the first Sitton to come into this area.

A Bill Stowe story about the Sitton and Gillespie families in *The Times-News*, a Hendersonville, North Carolina newspaper, begins,

The Gillespies couldn't have done it without the Sittons. And without the help of the Gillespie-Sitton family team, a lot of early settlers of Western North Carolina would have been without the tools and weapons they needed for survival.

This tale of Gillespies and Sittons spans the eighty years between the American Revolution and the Civil War. North Carolina was still pioneer country. The place where the two families became very necessary people now takes in Henderson and Transylvania counties, roughly one hundred miles west of Charlotte, twenty-five to thirty miles south and southwest of Asheville, and forty miles north of South Carolina's Greenville area[3].

---

[2] Author of <u>Look Homeward, Angel</u>.
[3] Where Greer is located.

In this stretch of wooded area where the Blue Ridge meets the Great Smokies, a rifle was man's indispensable friend. The Gillespies you see made rifles. Meat was 'on the hoof, on the paw and on the wing,' not at the supermarket. And between meals, scattered families of early settlers were constantly on guard against Indian marauders.

For a lot of reasons, a pioneer in the late 1700's and late 1800's needed iron. Whether he was clearing away forest, building a cabin, plowing a field, shoeing a horse or doing dozens of other jobs, a settler needed tools. He had no hardware store down the street, so he made the tools himself. That's where the Sittons come into the picture. The Sittons produced iron.

John Gillespie was a gunsmith and he and his wife, Jane Harvey Gillespie, settled at East Fork where he set up a gun shop. John and Jane had sons and daughters. This was about the turn of the 19th. century. Three sons followed in their father's trade and were gunsmiths.

The two girls were very knowledgeable when it came to their father's occupation. I dare say they never heard the term 'Equal Rights.' According to family records their mother held off a Cherokee raiding party and evidently she held an outdoor classroom for her daughters. It is reported that one of them was the best sharpshooter in their family. Her job was testing the Gillespie rifle for accuracy. Since the records do not tell us which of the two daughters this was, they both must have been experts in [the] art of survival.

Then Bert took us to meet Bob Gillespie. He was a tall, slender man who handled his Gillespie rifle as if he had grown up with it. A gracious host, he took pride in showing it to us.

It was five feet long and weighed about twelve pounds. Those made in the early 1800's are flintlocks with forty-four inch barrels and stocks of maple, walnut or cherry wood. The Gillespie rifle was not elaborate, it was practical and functional.

Bill Stowe, in his article, also tells us how the barrel was made and the guns loaded:

> To make a barrel, for example, the gunsmith heated thin iron bars until they were tractable, then bent them around a small iron rod. Finally he welded the edges of the bars together, a few inches at a time. If the barrel had to be enlarged, to produce a weapon of heavier caliber, he used a drill driven by a water wheel.
>
> The rifles were muzzle-loaders. First, the powder was put in through the barrel. Then wadding was packed in with a ramrod. Finally came the bullet, greased and wrapped in a 'patch of cloth'. Each hand-made gun had to have bullets made to its individual requirements.
>
> Gillespie rifles in the hands of collectors generally range between .45 and .46 caliber. The initials of Phillip Gillespie were on Bob Gillespie's rifle, the date was 1848. The piece of metal that came back into the stock was the Gillespie trademark. It was a muzzle-loader with a wooden stock.

To hold Bob's rifle in my hands while listening to him and Bert Sitton Jr. tell their stories was as close as one can get to a chapter of history. Sometimes I glance at or hold in my hand a piece of the "flag" from this old iron forge and I remember that

Sunday afternoon in the Blue Ridge Mountains.

Obviously Bob Gillespie did not want to part with his family rifle. I did not ask him about selling it.

CHAPTER 18

GOING FOR THE GOLD

Let me tell you something of how Louis L'Amour received the Congressional Gold Medal. It was Jack Evans of Jamestown, North Dakota who organized and participated in a national letter writing campaign to get this honor for L'Amour. Through tenacity and hard work his idea was crowned with success.

So who was Jack Evans? In his letter dated August 2, 1979 to the Honorable Jay S. Hammond, the governor of Alaska, Jack told this about his family:

My father, two uncles and my great-grandfather were part of the second Cheever Hazelet expedition that went up to claims on the Chisna and Chistochena in 1900. The group stayed two years and darned near starved to death and the gold return was so low the whole thing was a bust. But Dad was enchanted by Alaska and after returning to the states and marrying my mother, they went back up there where Dad was a forest ranger for awhile, then agent for the Alaska Steamship Company at Cardova. I was born on the dock at Cardova, as was a next younger brother, Dick. That dock was destroyed, by the way, in the big 1964 quake as were other parts of Cardova. A cousin, Craig

Hazelet, made available the land that new Valdez is situated on, when old Valdez was also put out of business by that big earthquake. I still have some relatives scattered around the fiftieth state.

At the fall meeting of the North Dakota Associated Press Association held in Devils Lake, two years after his retirement as editor of the *Jamestown Sun*, Jack Evans was recognized for his fifty years of work as a journalist. In presenting this award to Evans, the Jamestown Sun editor, James Smorada, described Evans as a "gentleman of uncommon courtesy."

The Jamestown Sun staff writer who covered this event summarized Evans' career as follows,

The Alaska native had worked in newspapers all across the country, worked on special computer projects for major California newspapers and wrote for two military publications during World War II. During the war Evans was stationed in North Africa and Europe.

The Jamestown Sun office is still located around the corner from our former business, the Hawkins Drug, now the Walz Drug. Over the years Jack and I visited during Chamber of Commerce committee meetings. We had the same interests in promoting tourism and the good quality of life found in this small city nestled along the junction of the James and Pipestem rivers. During these years I found Jack to be knowledgeable, quiet and comfortable to be around.

It was only after working with Jack on his idea of a Congressional Gold Medal for Louis L'Amour that I saw another of his talents. When he had an idea his tenacity surfaced. He never gave up.

On October 30, 1979, North Dakota Senator Milton Young introduced Senate Bill 1953. It was cosponsored by Senators Wallop, Burdick, Kassebaum, Thurmond, and Stevens.

" Be it enacted by the Senate and House of Representatives of the United States of America in Congress assembled,

(a) the President of the United States is authorized to present, on behalf of the Congress, to Louis L'Amour, a gold medal of appropriate design in recognition of his distinguished career as an author and his contributions to the Nation through his historically based works. For such purpose, the Secretary of the Treasury is authorized and directed to cause to be struck a gold medal with suitable emblems, devices, and inscriptions to be determined by the secretary of the Treasury. There are authorized to be appropriated not to exceed $15,000 to carry out the provisions of this subsection.

(b) The Secretary of the Treasury may cause duplicates in bronze of such medal to be coined and sold under such regulations as he may prescribe, at a price sufficient to cover the cost thereof, including labor, materials, dies, use of machinery, and overhead expenses, and the appropriation used for carrying out the provisions of this subsection shall be reimbursed out of the proceeds of such sale.

(c) The medals provided for in this Act are national medals for the purpose of section 3551 of the Revised Statutes (31 U.S.C. 368)."

In September 1983 my daughter Meredith sent me a clipping from The New York Times. It covered the scheduled presentation by President Reagan of a Congressional Gold Medal to Louis L'Amour. The New York Times writer, Edwin McDowell, first listed a number of past recipients of this award, then continued,

It is no derogation of Mr. L'Amour to point out that the award, however much it may be deserved, is heavily involved with politics, although often with nonpartisan politics. "That's why so few people have gotten the award," said Jack Evans of Jamestown, North

Dakota, who initiated the campaign on Mr. L'Amour's behalf and kept it going every time it began to falter.

Mr. Evans, a former California newspaper man, moved to Jamestown in 1969 and became editor of its daily newspaper, the Jamestown Sun. He met Mr. L'Amour, who was born in Jamestown, when the author was awarded an honorary degree at Jamestown College. As Mr. Evans became aware of Mr. L'Amour's worldwide popularity, he decided that the author deserved the medal, and he began lobbying North Dakota's Congressional delegation.

"A bill was pretty well along in Congress in 1979, but then John Wayne died, and they decided to give it to Wayne posthumously," Mr. Evans said. The 1980 elections derailed another bill. In addition, according to Mr. Evans, the Michigan Congressional delegation pledged support for Mr. L'Amour in return for North Dakota support for a medal for Joe Louis, the former heavyweight champion, while Pennsylvania wanted North Dakota's support for Fred Waring, the band leader.

The result of the horse-trading is that the boxer, the band leader and the western writer were all voted the medal last year.

When Jack first discussed this award it was something new to me. Without any hesitation my wife Margaret and I wholeheartedly supported him and became involved. By the time L'Amour's Gold Medal was presented by President Reagan at the White House on September 24, 1983, I felt I had a doctors degree in how to "Go for the Gold." Jack Evans was my professor.

In a June 13, 1988 article in *The Forum* (Fargo) telling of L'Amour's death, Jack was quoted, "I worked for three years writing more than 3000 personal letters to U. S. House and Senate members, to governors, to acquaintances in the publishing field and to many many fans of L'Amour. We were good friends. He was a pleasant person to know, a good husband and good father."

Jack, rounded up willing helpers, divided the US into sections. I was living in South Carolina so he asked me to concentrate on Georgia, South Carolina and North Carolina.

Those who mined for gold in the years Louis wrote about had problems. So did those who spearheaded the drive to secure this gold for L'Amour.

On March 20, 1980, Congressman Robert Garcia, chairman of the Committee on Post Office and Civil Service, wrote to Evans, "Thank you for writing to urge my support for legislation to strike a gold medallion in honor of Louis L'Amour.

"The Bill is currently pending in the Subcommittee on Consumer Affairs. I have been advised that the subcommittee has adopted a policy that no legislation will be moved without co-sponsorship of a majority of the Members of the House."

In a letter to Evans dated May 1, 1980, Senator Milton Young (ND) stated in part,

> If things go as scheduled, our bill making possible a medal for Louis L'Amour should be approved by the Senate Banking Committee by the middle of May or shortly thereafter. We shouldn't have much trouble on the Senate Floor either. Your efforts on this have been especially helpful and effective.
>
> The situation in the House appears to be more difficult. Getting approval of 218 members of the House won't be easy, but I don't think it will be impossible. It will require some work, though. I surely hope that we will succeed, as there is no one more deserving than Louis L'Amour. You may want to dis-

cuss the House situation personally with Congressman Andrews. The upcoming good publicity such as *The Readers Digest* and other publications will be very helpful, but it may be too late to get actions from both Houses of Congress unless we move as fast as we can now.

Jack it is amazing the number of people I run into almost daily who have read Louis L'Amour's books. Many of them not only have read all of them but have kept copies of them.

The following is the last portion of a communication to The Honorable William Proxmire, Chairman, Committee on Banking, Housing and Urban Affairs of the Senate from Deputy General Counsel of the Treasury Department. This was forwarded to Jack Evans by Senator Young's office on May 2, 1980.

The department recommends, however, that S.1953 be amended to increase the authorization ceiling provided therein. The Department notes that a presentational gold medal could not be produced at the cost of $15,000 as would be authorized in the proposed legislation. In terms of labor, overhead, and use of equipment alone, the process of preparing the design, models and master dies for the gold medal would cost an estimated $10,000 for the Bureau of the Mint which would design and strike the medal. In addition, since a presentational gold medal contains approximately fourteen ounces of gold, the metal value of the medal would be approximately $7,500, at the current market price of gold. Accordingly, the Department recommends that the amount authorized in subsection (a) of the proposed legislation be increased to $17,500.

"On the way to New York to visit our daughter Meredith," I wrote to L'Amour on July 14, 1981, "I spent one day visiting with personnel in the offices of ten senators about the Gold Medal for you. Bill Wright, a former editor of the *Jamestown Sun*, was working with Senator Andrews and I started with him and ended the day with a twenty to thirty minute conference with Linda Zemke."

She was a key person working with the Senate Banking Committee and she knew more about the original Senate Bill 1953 than all the others I talked with.

On September 18, 1981, answering my letter of inquiry, she sent me the following,

> The bill to give Louis L'Amour a gold medal was recently attached to a gold medal bill for Fred Waring. The legislative history is as follows:
>
> H.J. Res. 223, to give Fred Waring a gold medal, passed the House of Representatives in early August and was sent to the Senate, where it was referred to the Senate Banking Committee. When we received H.J. Res. 223, we amended it to provide for a gold medal to Louis L'Amour, upon the request of Senator Armstrong of Colorado. Apparently, Mr. L'Amour now lives in Durango, Colorado.[1]
>
> It was also amended to provide a gold medal for the widow of the boxing champion Joe Lewis, as requested by Senator Riegle. H.J. Res. 223, thus amended, passed the Senate Banking Committee and the full Senate on September 15th and was sent back to the House of Representatives. As of yesterday it was being 'held at the desk' on the floor of the House of Representatives and had not been referred back to the House Banking Committee.

---

[1] L'Amour lived in Los Angeles but spent the month of August each year in the Durango, Colorado area.

At this point, the Senate has, for the <u>second</u> time, passed the Louis L'Amour gold medal bill and sent it to the House for consideration. Hopefully they will pass H.R. Res. 223, and Mr. L'Amour will get his well-deserved medal.

I was delighted to hear from you again.

Once a gold medal is given to an individual the Bureau of the Mint issues a finely detailed duplicate struck in bronze, in this case ninety percent copper, ten percent zinc. These are sold by mail or over the counter. All proceeds from sales, after reimbursements for costs, are deposited to the General Fund of the United States.

Before Louis L'Amour was voted this medal, only eighty had been awarded by our Congress. George Washington was the first to receive this distinctive recognition.

Jack Evans received many answers from L'Amour fans saying they had written letters to their House members and Senators in support of this project. He told us he had been in touch with all who replied to his initial request for assistance saying,

"They are doing a fantastic job writing their own senators and congressmen as well as some outside their own districts. The most any one of them had written was sixty letters, many in the range of from ten to twenty."

This project started by Jack Evans of Jamestown, ND would never have been successful if it weren't for the response from L'Amour's fans. Samples from those who took time to express their thoughts and feelings follow,

Your letter requesting support for a National Gold Medal for Louis L'Amour made my heart soar like a hawk! My first letter ever to a US Senator is enclosed. I can think of no other effort I would more heartily endorse.

You are so right that I am an admirer of Mr. L'Amour. I am a fifth generation Oregonian relating straight back to Jim Bridger. To my knowledge no printed word by Mr. L'Amour has escaped me. I could go on so! (Greg J. Baker, February 27, 1980.)

Mr. Baker also told Jack of his interest in L'Amour's planned town of Shalako near Durango. In 1978, he heard that L'Amour planned an annual trip to Durango in August.

After 3 days of "camping" at the San Juan Club (Tamarron) for breakfast, I did meet Mr. L'Amour. No momentous occasion for Mr. L'Amour, but assuredly one for me! I will not forget it. The previous day was Mr. L'Amour's birthday. The officials of Mesa Verde National Park had invited him to the park after closing at night. Their birthday offering was to light small fires, on signal, in each of the Cliff dwellings. What a thrilling sight! I won't forget Mr. L'Amour's stirring account of this and his classic statement. "It must have been just the way it was."

I am so happy to be a part of your effort! Thanks so much for asking for my help.

Joe McKeever, pastor of the First Baptist Church, Columbus, MS wrote, "I've written a half-dozen letters to Senators and Congressmen on Mr. L'Amour regarding the well-deserved medal. Thanks for thinking of it. I passed your letter on to another fan who told me two days later he had already written thirty letters.

"I occasionally quote Louis L'Amour in my sermons. He stands for many of the same things the Bible does — integrity, work, strength, courage. Thanks for what you are doing."

A handwritten note from Mrs. Maude Potter, February 26, 1980.

"I have read many of his books and have a personal letter

from him. I live at this Old Folks Home, am ninety-five [years old] and have no addresses to whom to write. Please give me a complete list – No matter how many – I'll write each one."

Marijane Morris of Hemet, California wrote this letter to Senator Alan Cranston, February 28, 1980. A copy was sent to Jack Evans.

This bill deserves attention. I know at first hand what his novels can do in a classroom. In the age of obscene language, cowardly "heroes", violence on innocent beings, violence without reason, disrespect, dishonesty everywhere, and other dreadful happenings we seem powerless to control, he gives my students honesty, cleanness, clearness and models. All of this and more is placed in a background of history and places that are authentic. I know that when I place one of his books in the hand of one of my students, I have done him a service and a favor that becomes infinite.

I have spent most of my teaching career, here in Hemet, California teaching so called reluctant readers.

One "show me" student, after reading just one of Mr. L'Amour's novels, then read thirty-five as if he were starving for what they had to offer. Another student stopped by my desk one day and said, "Mrs. Morris, I see lots of little flakes carrying and reading Louis L'Amour. They have been turned on!"

I could write you several pages of appreciation for the novels of this great Western writer. One more example: The reading does not stop with the classroom and that is what reading is all about. It also ripples out into the home because students ask if they might take a book home for Dad, or for Grandfather.

Lee Ridgway from Fargo, ND expressed his thoughts to Senator Quinton Burdick,

Not being a native North Dakotan or westerner, I believe I particularly appreciate and admire the "code" that is the cardinal theme in each of his works. The quality of the "ordinary" people he describes, such as self reliance, determination to succeed in the face of great odds, courage, strength (both physical and moral) are the attributes I believe constitute the fiber of our people and our country.

Mr. L'Amour's simply stated philosophy of a strong people tells what we Americans are made of, from where we have come and what we have done in the face of all kinds of adversity. I would urge <u>every</u> American, young and old, to read Mr. L'Amour's messages through his many tales of the West. I intend to reread each of his books and have recommended them to my friends and associates.

Congressman Lionel Van Deerlin from District 42 of California wrote to Jack, "I got quite a lot of encouragement on this matter from my administrative assistant who proudly claims herself as the daughter of the Dakota Prairie."

Then North Dakota's Harold Schafer[2] capsulized his thoughts in a note to Senator Nancy Kassebaum, "All the world loves a good cowboy. No question but that Louis L'Amour has created more good cowboys than any other human being. Thank you for being a part of the introduction of Senate Bill No. 1953."

By the time L'Amour's Gold Medal was presented to him by President Reagan at the White House on September 24, 1983, thousands had participated in this effort. During the presentation President Reagan and Louis L'Amour stood in the foreground while a group of rodeo riders were spaced in a half-circle behind them.

---

[2] Founder of Gold Seal Company.

As Louis looked down at the medal in his hand he saw an excellent portrait of himself. The reverse side was inscribed, "The Dream in the Mind — Realization in the Hand."

Suppose, when I stroll across a meadow, follow a trail in the hills, or walk along the edge of a stream, I bend over from time to time and pick up a nugget of gold. Then I examine it and toss it under a bush or into the stream knowing there are many more along the trail.

Value is a relative thing. If gold were as plentiful as the shells along the seashore, it would not be worth $300 to $400 an ounce. Congress had to thoughtfully and carefully examine the qualifications of this nominee for a gold medal, review in detail his accomplishments, determine if he, through excelling in his chosen field, had significantly contributed to the lives of his readers.

Those who read L'Amour carved their names on a chair in his classroom. It is they who judged his value. And it is from their letters to Congress that our legislators gained a sense of the value of L'Amour's writing and his contribution to the history of our frontier.

CHAPTER 19

REACHING THE JAMES

First came the trickle of explorers who challenged the frontier that lay west of their tree-covered hills and mountains. They wanted to see what lay in the vast country beyond the setting sun. Familiar surroundings became memories by the time they reached the Mississippi River.

I have stood on the bank of the Mississippi at its beginning near Bemidji, Minnesota and have watched it disappear into the gulf at New Orleans. It is amazing to me that something which starts as an inconsequential creek becomes a mighty conduit with a will of its own.

From diaries and journals we learn of the struggle of these early explorers who day after day, month after month, moved beyond this great river and into the center of, what was to them, an endless open prairie. To most it was a long agonizing wasteland, thought of as a large forbidden desert unsuitable for cultivation or general habitation..

In Louis L'Amour's novel Lonely on the Mountain we have an excellent description of the land through which an early cattle drive took place during the middle of the 1870's. Tell Sackett was moving a herd of 1100 cattle up from the South into Dakota territory. There were long monotonous days on the trail. Some winter

148

snow still remained on the shady slopes and patches of green grass were just beginning to appear after a long winter of sleep. The cattle had to feed on the brown cured grass from the previous summer.

At one of their camp locations Cap Rountree placed his tin cup of coffee on the ground near the camp fire. He picked up a small dead branch, snapped off the end and began drawing a map in the sand. As he was doing this, he said,

> Right here's where we are. Right over here is the Jim River —the James if you want to be persnickety about it. I say we drive west, then follow the Jim north, which gives us water all the way.
>
> Right here there's a mighty pretty valley where the Pipestem flows into the Jim. We can let the cattle have a day there, which will give Orrin a chance to gain on us.
>
> There's good grass in that valley, and there's a lot of elm, box elder, and some cottonwood along the rivers. There'll be firewood and shade for the stock if we have to wait, and it might pay to wait a couple of days for Orrin.[1]

I know the James River well. Early this morning after getting a cup of coffee, I walked to the door leading to our patio. I looked out and a few feet beyond the fence rail edging the patio was the James River. It was springtime in North Dakota. Against the current of this swiftly moving water three pair of wood ducks effortlessly made their way north.

This is the same Jim River Cap Rountree was talking about and the "mighty pretty valley" he describes is now the location of Jamestown, North Dakota, the town where Louis L'Amour was born and grew up.

About the same time Cap was drawing his map in the sand,

---

[1] Lonely on the Mountain, chapter 2.

Orrin Sackett was following along the bank of the Red River moving north. Instead of a pack horse his party was using a Red River cart.

"Each cart was about six feet long and three wide; the bottom was of one-inch boards; the wheels were seven and a half feet in diameter. The hubs were ten inches across and bored to receive an axle of split oak. The wood used was oak throughout. Each cart was drawn by a single horse and would carry approximately four hundred pounds. No nails were used. Oak pins and rawhide bindings held it together."[2]

Orrin and his party crossed Rice Creek and continued on to Georgetown. After a brief stop they moved on for about twenty miles where they boarded The International, a sternwheeler powered by two steam boilers, which was moored along the bank. Their immediate destination was Pembina from where they would enter Canada and start westward to join Tell and his herd of cattle.

Maynard Stephens of Ronan, Montana, an accomplished photographer, writer and wood carver, now has one of his riverboat models, the *Rosebud*, on display in the North Dakota Heritage Center.

In a publication given to me by Jamestown resident Glen Divers, the Rosebud was described as "another Coulson product from Pennsylvania – a busy workhorse on the Yellowstone throughout its career, a sizable craft and considered one of the finest boats on the river. She was one hundred ninety-three feet long, thirty-three feet wide and had a hold three feet six inches deep, giving her a capacity of two hundred eighty-six net tonnage. As part of the Coulson line of steamers her seven-character name was in accord with other members of the clan, the most famous of which was the Josephine, which broke the seven-digit rule, Far West, Key West, Western, Montana, Wyoming and Dakotah. They represented about one-third of all steamboats operating on the Yellowstone in 1877."[3]

---

[2] Lonely on the Mountain, chapter 8.
[3] "Hoof Prints" Yellowstone Corral of the Westerners, Spring-Summer, 1993.

Many changes have taken place since the time when L'Amour's story <u>Lonely on the Mountain</u> was set. Pioneers moved in from the East and farmers brought plows with them. The dark soil was exposed as the horses pushed forward on their collars. Rolls of sod cast straight early morning shadows on the flat virgin grass. Lines of the harness were draped around the plowman's neck. Beads of perspiration rose on his face before trickling downward.

This was the beginning of our state as we know it. Water was sought and found. Sod houses rose upon the plains and cattle ranged across the open prairie.

Then there were the riverboats. In 1874 the Josephine, flagship of the Yellowstone, described as a majestic river queen, made its first of forty trips to Fort Benton on the Missouri. Sternwheelers earned their place in the story of frontier development. Next came the railroads and more homesteaders followed searching for a new and free life.

Remembering those years, what can the old-timers today tell their great-grandchildren? How can they pass this knowledge on to those who have never seen horses pulling a plow or a blacksmith sharpening one?

CHAPTER 20

BREAKING NEW GROUND

On October 9, 1976 a group of North Dakotans from all over the state gathered on the grounds of our state capital in Bismarck. A new and different kind of ground-breaking was to take place, this time with shovels instead of a plow. North Dakota was to have a Heritage Center.

Louis L'Amour had called to tell us he had accepted an invitation to be the main speaker at this ground-breaking event. We got in touch with our son, Allan, an attorney in Cooperstown, North Dakota, and daughter Meredith, an art and creative writing teacher in Chaska, Minnesota, a suburb of Minneapolis, to tell them the good news.

Allan planned to join us.

"I'm so sorry," Meredith wrote, "I won't be joining you for the big day in North Dakota. I know I would have enjoyed it! There always seems to be more to do at school than I manage to get done. On Tuesday those of us who are working with the deaf children will begin classes in sign language.

"It's fun to be doing art with the kids. They are doing extremely well on the still life. Did I tell you I had picked up some interesting objects at Salvation Army? The boys are particularly turned on by the football items and most of the girls are including the old doll and the copper boiler. They may have picked up a little about those antiques in the process.

"Well, once again I am sorry I won't be joining you in Bismarck!"

It had been four years since we first greeted the L'Amour family in Jamestown and showed their children, Beau and Angelique, the town where their dad grew up. Now we were to host Louis for his stay in Bismarck.

It was a beautiful clear day when L'Amour's flight landed in Bismarck. Allan and I were there to greet him. Margaret and I were glad our son would get to know this interesting friend of ours. Meredith had the same opportunity in 1975 when she and I flew to my hometown of Greer, South Carolina to meet the L'Amours on a research trip which began in Washington, DC.

The next day Allan, his family, Margaret, her mother Sigga Benson and I ate beef stew from Mary Young's[1] chuck wagon, viewed the 6th Infantry Encampment and saw the sod turned over at the site of the proposed heritage center. During the day's activities Allan took pictures – some now treasures in our L'Amour Collection.

In the early afternoon after an introduction by the master of ceremonies State Senator Bob Melland of Jamestown, Louis L'Amour stood at the podium. The waiting crowd settled down to quietly listen. He began,

> I think I could do much better up here if I had a typewriter. I am more used to it. In the first place I want to tell you about my feelings for North Dakota. I left here a long time ago, never left here in spirit. I have always felt like a North Dakotan and I still do, probably always will. My family has been connected with the state in one way or another for over a hundred years.

[1] Mary Young is a Jamestown historian and an old friend of ours, a newer friend of Louis'.

My great-grandfather was killed by the Sioux out here about fifty miles from Jamestown and was buried out there for a short time. His body now lies in Sioux Falls. He was fighting for what he believed and no doubt the Indians who killed him were also. I had a grandfather who was with the Sibley Command at the same time and he came back to North Dakota in 1881. He moved his family out here in 1883, then they moved to Jamestown from Carrington in 1884. My family in one way or another have been connected to the state ever since. If we haven't lived here we were always here in spirit.

My sister, Edna LaMoore Waldo, whom some of you know, used to live here in Bismarck for a long time, wrote a book called <u>Dakota</u> which is the history of Dakota Territory – still one of the best. So my connections here are very deep and I feel very much at home here with all of you.

I was very glad to have a chance to come back and speak on this occasion. To me there has been no more important occasion since the beginning of this country than this bicentennial. The original birthday of our country of course is important but now we are celebrating two hundred years of success.

There have been those who contrive our so-called success and haven't believed in it. They point to things we haven't done which perhaps we should have done but, nevertheless, in two hundred years we have built here a great nation that holds its place among all the great nations of history of all times, in all places.

The men and women who built this country came here from Europe. They came from other places, they came from all the continents of the world and they came here alone and of their own initiative. Since the beginning of time there have been migrations across the face of the earth. People have moved. They moved out of Asia and across Europe, down to the shores of Europe and all these migrations were directed by a king or an emperor of some sort, except the migration to the United States and the migration westward after the United States was born.

In this case it was a matter of individual voli- tion. Each individual chose for himself to come. He was not told to come. Many people of like economic status stayed where they were, others came here. What was the difference? What was the fact that made some come and made others stay? Why did some stay back east and others come west?

I think there is something deep in the genes of those people who came west that made them want to explore, that made them want to venture to a new coun- try, that made them willing to take a chance. It has long been thought that those men who came west did so simply because they were poor, because they wanted land. Many of them left good businesses behind, many left good farms, many left good life behind and came west simply because they wanted to come to a new country, to the new country.

They came out here, they came to North Da- kota, they came to other places in the west and they established themselves here. They had a lot to learn on the way west. For a hundred and fifty years or more Americans had pioneered in the Eastern states. Mostly it was a matter of cutting down trees, clearing land, building log cabins using the trees they cut down. They learned how to pioneer, they knew how it should be done.

Then they crossed the Mississippi and came west and a whole new world opened up before them, a kind of a world they hadn't seen before. Out here was the vast plains country, miles upon miles of grass, miles upon miles of great sky and endless horizon. Moving westward on covered wagons, on horseback, some people on foot, they traveled very slowly at an average of perhaps twelve miles a day – some a little bit faster and some much slower.

To them that march westward was endless. They went on day after day, day after day. At first they walked in fear and trembling, they weren't sure. They had courage or they wouldn't have come in the first place. But they came west, hesitating a little bit because they didn't know the problems they were going to face. But they came westward and as they moved they changed.

I have read many of their diaries and many of their journals, I have read the letters they wrote back home. I spent a great part of my life researching the history of these people. I know a good deal about how they thought and felt. It is not imagination with me because I have read their own words and I have heard them express themselves.

They weren't sure of themselves at first, but then they began to overcome the obstacles. They crossed the streams, some of them flooded, they got through the hail storms, they endured the dust storms, they fought the Indians, they made their way slowly westward.

Suddenly a change came over them. You can see the change in their diaries and journals and I have read many of them. You can see the change taking place and they began to feel it isn't so tough. I can do it. And from that came the feeling I can do anything. And that's why we put a man on the moon.

But these westward moving people had had only one thing in their minds, two things perhaps. Some of them wanted to make money. One fellow's diary I read said he wanted to get rich and get out. As a matter of fact he didn't. He came west, fell in love with the land and stayed.

But most of them wanted homes. Most of them wanted to build. They came west into a wild and rough country. Usually the first things that opened were saloons and gambling houses. But right shortly after came the churches and schools because the people who came west were building a civilization, a civilization that would last, a civilization that would give much to the world.

When we started moving into this country, we had great problems. We had left Europe behind us, a Europe that had a strong caste system that allowed very small chance for an individual to advance. He had a chance but it was very slight and mostly through warfare. They came west to open up a new country, they wanted to get rid of all the sort of thing they left behind them. They wanted this to be new, they wanted to be different, they wanted to be free.

Now all over the country we have that freedom and we are keeping that freedom. Where there was wide open barren plains we plowed the land, we built homes, we fed half the world and we continue to feed half the world. We feed it not only from our land, but with our energies and from our heart.

I live in California now and a short time ago a terrible hurricane hit Baja California, a part of Mexico. Within a matter of hours after the hurricane stopped blowing, Americans were on the ground with food, medicines and other help. And so it has been always and everywhere. We have done that with every country that needed help that was open to us. We refused nobody, even people who are sometimes our enemies. This is good, this is the way it should be.

This is also reflected in the pioneer spirit. When men came west no man could really stand alone. They had the courage to do it, the strength to do it and in many cases they had to do it for a short time. But when men built a cabin, built a barn, the neighbors came over to help. When they had to thresh the neighbors came over to help. It was always a matter of one helping another. They became a cooperative society. An individualist society, but one that was also very cooperative. They knew how to help one another and so we know how to help other nations and we do it. And I am proud we can do it and that we go on doing it.

When a man climbs a mountain, he reaches a point in his climbing where he strikes a little level space and he stops and turns around and looks the country over to see where he is going, to see where he has got to go. But he also looks back to see where he has been and it is very important that he do that. It is very important that every once in a while we stop and take stock of our position and see what we have done and from where we have come.

The heritage center that is going to be built here in this area will give us a good chance to do that. It will show us some of the artifacts, some of the material that was used here. We will get a chance to look at them, see how our ancestors fought the country, made the country, lived in the country and see how they got along. We get a good chance to see what we have done and the distance we have come. That's only important so long as we realize it's only preliminary to the distance we've got to go. This is only a landing place, the greatest fight still lies ahead of us.

One question I am often asked from my readers or when I am talking at places like this is, "Do we have that feeling yet?" and I definitely answer. "Yes."

I have known many of those old timers, I have worked with them, talked with them. I had the opportunity when I was a little boy of hearing my grandfather tell stories. I had a chance to meet some of the old Indians he fought with in battles. I had a chance to sit around and listen. Very little of that do I remember because I was too young, but nevertheless I remember the overall effect.

Since then, in traveling around the country, I have known thirty-five to forty of the old gun fighters and outlaws. I have known hundreds of the old pioneers. I have sat with them and talked with them. I have sat on their porch when the sunlight is on them.

This was in New Mexico. I have listened to an old woman tell stories about Billy the Kid, the night he was going to be killed. I heard her tell all about it. I have talked to these people so I know what they are like. I'm not dreaming this. It is not something that just comes out of my head. I have read, as I have said, their diaries. I have talked to them. They were strong gutsy people, they were people who rose to emergencies. And I have had an opportunity in my lifetime to see some of us rise to these same emergencies.

I served in the army in World War II and I saw boys come over there with no experience in battle who showed themselves very brave, very courageous, as good as any man who ever walked. So I say the old blood is still here, the old feeling is still here and you need have no doubt about it, we could do today just as they did then, whatever is necessary to secure the future.

There is much that lies before us. Pioneering has just begun. You have heard a lot of talk about science fiction, about outer space. It is here right now. We will be having relatives out there before very long. We have all the expertise, all the knowledge necessary to establish colonies in space right now. We don't need to do another thing, and we will be out there doing it. I am very sure that when those colonies are first established and people get going out there, people from North Dakota will be out there among the first.

The world we live in changes from day to day but some things remain the same. I think one of the reasons for my success, selling the number of books I have, is because I remember that. I remember there are certain virtues that are important, certain basic moral standards are important.

I have much difficulty from time to time with motion pictures made from my books because some of the people want to change them, they want to alter them. Unhappily when you sell a story you have no further control over it. The new people can do what they want.

Now because of the reputation I have acquired, they do come to me and ask questions. Too many of them want to change the attitudes they had in those days to some of the attitudes that are current now. I won't stand for it because of what was different then in that respect. They had different attitudes toward church, different attitude toward almost everything.

Some of those attitudes still prevail. I hope they will continue to prevail everywhere. These people had courage, they had strength, they had endurance, they had a very strong belief in what they believed, they really had strong beliefs in their moral attitude, in their political attitudes. They often fought over politics. They don't do that so much any more and it is probably just as good, but nevertheless it showed they were involved and they were very much involved.

I am not going to keep you here very long . . . do a lot of talking. I don't want to keep you here sitting in the sunlight while I tell a lot of stories. Our country has endured a great deal without having to endure speakers who speak too long.

But we have suffered almost everything. We have been through wars, passed through some revolutions and we have endured and that is the quality we must all remember. We have endured, we can endure.

Now we are facing a new future, a different kind of a future, and I know we will face up to it just as we have the others in the past. This heritage center that is going to be established here on this ground will be a place where we can go and look and see what we have done, where over the years we can continue to leave the artifacts that will record our history.

The important thing to remember is that history is not something that happened just a long time ago. History is happening today. We are making history. Each one of you is making history. Each one of you is a part of history. All of you must think of that, you must keep it in mind when you vote. I know there are a lot of people these days who don't vote. I am glad to say this is not true of North Dakotans. I am sure everyone here in this state who is of legal voting age will be voting at the polls when the time comes to go to the polls, because that's how it was all built and that's how we can keep it all.

I want to thank you very much for inviting me here to talk to you today. It has been a real pleasure. I am glad we had such a warm beautiful day. I am sure this was due to Governor Link and his cohorts who helped him. I know they wouldn't allow a bad day to happen because we all have to sit here in the open. I want to thank you very much for honoring me by having me come here to speak to you. Thank you.

Later that afternoon Margaret and I attended a reception given in L'Amour's honor at the Governor's mansion. My introduction of L'Amour was cut short by Margaret, who said the people were there to hear Louis.

When I saw Louis off on his return flight to Los Angeles I knew many of those who listened to his presentation would have a new and better understanding of the elements, the hardships, and loneliness – and yes, even the joys of a new beginning in a land called the Dakotas.

CHAPTER 21

200 MILLION AND COUNTING

There are books written for children and books written for adults that can be recommended reading for children. The latter is unusual and I have never failed to stress this in the talks I've made about Louis L'Amour to adult groups. There are many children who have developed an interest in reading because someone introduced them to one of L'Amour's books.

Because of our personal relationship with Louis and his family and my knowledge of what he wrote, we have, over the years, shared our stories and thoughts about L'Amour with many others. During a time when publishers and readers were thriving on offensive words and scenes, L'Amour wrote stories free of such, yet achieved success almost unheard of in the publishing world.

One day Marion Morris, an English teacher at Jamestown Junior High School, called me. She had begun a summer school class in literature for a group of seventh grade children who had experienced trouble with the course during the regular school session.

She told me she started her class each day by reading one chapter of L'Amour's <u>Down the Long Hills</u>. Here was a teacher who turned a key, unlocking a door for this group of kids. She was delighted with their response. Her enthusiasm, excitement if you will, gave me a warm feeling.

"Some in the class pleaded for me to read two chapters a day instead of the one," she said. At her request I became a visiting teacher for an hour, telling stories about Louis L'Amour and answering questions. These stories about L'Amour's life in Jamestown, and during his wandering years after leaving his hometown, were just as appealing to them as was the story of the survival of two children in <u>Down The Long Hills</u>.

At some later date I joined Anne Olafson's senior class studying <u>Sitka</u>, L'Amour's story of the purchase of Alaska. I shared with them some of our experiences when we were Louis' guests on trips to actual places he wrote about in his books.

In 1976 the Jamestown School Board approved a request by Dr. Keith Prentice, member of the Curriculum Committee, to incorporate books written by Louis L'Amour into their course of study. During the discussion Superintendent Frank Fischer quoted from a letter I had written to him:

"I believe the exposure given to students who read L'Amour's works under this program will be very meaningful. Surely all present and future students will have a better understanding of their country and those individual pioneers who participated in the movement of the frontier from the Eastern shore to the Western boundary of this land."

The following books were chosen to be studied the first year:

7th Grade: <u>Down the Long Hills</u>
8th Grade: <u>Over on the Dry Side</u>
9th Grade: <u>Sackett's Land</u>
Sophomore: <u>The Ferguson Rifle</u>
Junior-Senior: <u>Sitka</u>

Jack Evans quoted L'Amour in his editorial column *Buffalo Territory*, in the March 11, 1977 issue of the *Jamestown Sun*:

I spent hours after school and during my vacations, reading from many books. We had books at home, and we had belonged to the library from its first foundation, but this was not enough. I shall never forget my excitement when I discovered non-fiction could be as exciting as fiction.

I had read most of the boys' books available, and then started on Alexander Dumas. The library had a set of his works in, I believe, about forty volumes. I read them all. From my reading I began to realize there were many things of which I knew nothing, and I had better start learning.

The first book of more serious reading, and I remember it well, was a battered volume called <u>The Genius of Solitude</u>, and it contained a chapter on Socrates. I was thirteen years when he became one of my heroes, and he still is. My next was an excellent book on Natural Science, and I wish I could buy it today. This led me to books on botany, geology, mineralogy and chemistry. There was a series of <u>Life In Town and Country</u> books, on each country. I began with India. This led me to a large book where I bogged down. It was <u>India, Under Curzon and After</u>. I never completed it.

Many the nights I read until the library closed and I have continued to read in libraries ever since in all parts of the world.

The marvel of the world in which we live, a greater marvel than radio, television or space flight, is how easily obtainable are the great books. We can in our libraries, in our own homes, on planes, trains or buses, listen to the words of the greatest thinkers of all time. We can share their thoughts, their troubles, know their disappointments as well as their achievements.

In February of 1989, upon receiving word that the Jamestown School Board was considering naming its new school after Louis L'Amour, Margaret, in a letter to the board, expressed appreciation for their civic efforts, particularly their many hours of work for the school system.

For years we had felt there should be visible evidence in Jamestown to recognize L'Amour as one who always remembered with fondness and appreciation his boyhood days in this small city. Our thinking was that to associate him with a new elementary school would be something appreciated by his readers everywhere.

In her letter to the school board Margaret described Louis as "a terrific individual, outstanding in character, personality, ability and appearance.

"He has become a household word since we left Jamestown eleven years ago and is very popular here in South Carolina. His large print books are numerous in libraries and are in big demand. How better could your school board honor someone who has, through his books, made Jamestown, North Dakota a household word in millions of homes across our country?"

At this time nearly two hundred million books were in print and his works had been translated into twenty languages.

On June 14, 1989, nearly one year after his death, the Jamestown School Board named their newest elementary school after Louis L'Amour. This was the first new school to open in Jamestown since 1965.

Board member Jim Madsen had proposed the name earlier in the year. He headed a committee which reviewed five other names. One of his comments was, "The Louis L'Amour name suits the new school because it pays tribute to a Jamestown native, and because the writer could serve as a role model to children."

Jan Odin, who chaired the dedication committee commented,

"Students at the school have been studying Louis L'Amour's history and his books. The task has been made easier with the presentation of two complete sets of L'Amour's books to the school library by the L'Amour Family."

So during the years ahead, there will be children entering the Louis L'Amour School for the first time. They will learn to read and my hope is, as they grow older, many will read his books and get to know the man for whom their school was named, for his thinking is reflected in the lives of the characters in his books.

Were Louis alive today, knowing him as I did, he would value the naming of this school after him as much as any of the many honors he received during his lifetime. In a sense he has returned to his childhood home and will walk the halls along with children who will be our future leaders.

168

CHAPTER 22

IN PASSIONATE PURSUIT OF KNOWLEDGE

"The school is rapidly nearing completion," Ralph Kraft[1] wrote us on May 31, 1990. "Our school board has toured the building twice and we are very pleased with the facility. It is functional and attractive without being extravagant. It will contain seven classrooms and a library in which we plan to have a section honoring Louis L'Amour. There will also be a gymnasium which doubles as a lunch room, plus offices and an area for special education. The design is such that it will be easy to add on when needed.

"On behalf of the Jamestown School Board and its committee for the dedication, I want to extend to you and Mrs. Hawkins our invitation to join us for this event. I will advise you of the date as soon as it is confirmed."

When Mr. Kraft later confirmed the date, he told us the Dedication Committee wanted me to introduce Mrs. L'Amour at the ceremony. She would be giving the dedicatory address.

Those who did so much to make that September 30th a memorable day started long before the dedication began. The weather was in the seventies. A blue sky with scattered clouds made it a typical North Dakota early fall day.

Arriving first, the teachers and staff greeted the children, their parents, the honored guests and others who came to join in cel-

---

[1] Former English teacher at Jamestown High School, serving on the school board.

ebrating the occasion. When principal Jake Wolf began his opening remarks, every seat in the gymnasium was filled and some individuals stood in the rear. His podium was on a platform especially constructed for the occasion.

Three saddles were spaced along a two foot high wooden railing. Between them saddle blankets and a buffalo robe were draped. On the center post was a large black western hat with the front brim facing the audience, on two other posts were bridles.

Centered on the floor in front of the elevated platform was a large wagon wheel leaning against several bales of hay, at its base a buffalo skull. Spaced on each side were two additional stacks of baled hay. Pumpkins were arranged in front and on top of them.

Behind the platform in large black letters on the pale blue wall was:

WELCOME TO
LOUIS L'AMOUR
SCHOOL

On either side of this greeting was a black silhouette of a bronco-buster in action, his right hand grasping the saddle horn. His left, holding his hat, was raised high above his head.

The children of Louis L'Amour School had chosen the lobo[2] as their mascot. One was depicted in black silhouette against a full moon on the right wall. His head was pointed skyward, his yowling mouth wide open. The western theme did credit to this writer of frontier stories.

Several times Louis had told me, "Many look but they fail to see." L'Amour usually grasped the details and vividly recalled them at a future date. So, as I stood in the quiet of the gymnasium before the activities started, I knew he would have valued the details and work needed to create the scene before me.

After Mr. Wolf introduced me, I approached the podium to

---

[2] Timber wolf

introduce Kathy L'Amour. I was appearing before a group of friends, for we had lived with the people of Jamestown for twenty-one years. During those years we saw our two children move through the elementary, junior and senior high schools.

A thought or two about my wife, Margaret. I think of her as a "Down to Earth" ambassador for North Dakota. Wherever we have lived and in our travels, she has planted a good image of her state and its people. She is one of you, a North Dakota native.

These "images" she has planted have grown, blossomed and thrived, helping to change opinions of those who only know North Dakota as an "Ice Box" from where escape is the only thing.

My ambassadorial activities have been but echoes of her ideas, thoughts and suggestions. I thank her for introducing me to Jamestown many years ago.

We are glad to be back home. We have very good and special memories of those years here. Thank you all for inviting us back.

Margaret and I have been in book stores from the East Coast to the West, from the North to the South. All of them feature a section of books written by Louis L'Amour. His birthplace, Jamestown, North Dakota is mentioned in each paperback.

We have been particularly interested in his readers with whom we have had personal visits. Here is a sampling of them:

Dr. Linda Lucas, professor at the graduate college of Library and Information Science, University of South Carolina, is an avid reader of L'Amour's frontier stories.

Ruth Frazier, from Oak Ridge, Tennessee, a high school English Literature and World History teacher, made an in-depth study of L'Amour's writings after her retirement. She believed she discovered in his works a new form of writing which she called "prose-poetry".

Val Wirth, a librarian in Braddon, Australia says, 'I would stand on the top of Sydney Harbor bridge and sell his works if it would spread the word.'

I recall a nurse's aid at the Greenville, South Carolina Memorial Hospital. What a thrill for her when she found that Margaret and I were personal friends of L'Amour. On my visit the following day I brought a picture of Louis for her to see. She then rushed out of the room returning shortly with Dr. Hyde, an orthopedic surgeon. He told me the whole direction of his life changed after reading Louis L'Amour.

Among these and many more was Hazel D. Wright of Chasley, North Dakota who wrote me at our drug store requesting a complete list of his books so she could order the ones she did not have. She ended with, "I am 81 years old and I don't have much time."

We will never know how much enjoyment, how much knowledge, and how many lives have been changed because of what this writer has left in the minds and hearts of the myriad of people who have read his works.

Why do I speak of Louis and his readers when I am here to present his wife, Kathy? It's because she played such an important role in his life and career.

Margaret and I first met the L'Amour Family (Louis, Kathy, Angelique and Beau) in 1972. Many times since then we have been guests in their home.

We spent one week with them in Durango, Colorado. On another occasion, I traveled with them for a week on a 'Research-Vacation' through the Blue Ridge Mountains from South Carolina to Washington, DC.

I am happy to have this chance to express our feelings about those enjoyable, unforgettable occasions. Margaret and I thank you, Kathy.

I know of no better way to introduce Kathy L'Amour than to move back the calendar and read from an article I wrote that was published fifteen years ago in the 1975 Spring Edition of *The North Dakota Horizons.* My thoughts about Kathy today are the same as they were then:

"For nineteen years Louis has shared his successes with his wife Kathy. She was born in Los Angeles, attended Westlake School for Girls and the University of Southern California. She was a talented successful actress who voluntarily gave up her career when they were married. This was the first marriage for both of them. Through the years Kathy devoted all her time to her husband, children and home. She is a beautiful woman, versatile, knowledgeable, creative—a delightful person whose happiness is reflected in the faces of their daughter, Angelique and son, Beau. Louis said of Kathy, 'She is a major part of every aspect of my life.' "

Kathy, on behalf of Jamestown, its school board and those present here today, we welcome you and thank you for sharing your presence to celebrate this outstanding occasion.

Thank you, Reese. What an honor this is for us

today. I'm only sorry that my son Beau and my daughter Angelique couldn't be here to experience this with me. But Angelique just got married a week ago and she is off on her honeymoon and Beau has to work, so here I am by myself to do the best I can.

Louis would have been so pleased to have this beautiful school in Jamestown named for him. I remember when he brought Beau and Angelique and me to Jamestown for the very first time. It was like a dream come true. The town turned out for us in such an incredible way.

We landed late at night and there was a large crowd at the airport – huge bouquets of lilacs for Angelique and me, the kind we'd hardly seen before, and a mounted sheriff's posse and a banner saying,

Welcome Home Louis L'Amour

Everyone was so warm and friendly, we just couldn't get over it. The shops all had copies of his books in the windows. And the children were swept up in Reese and Margaret Hawkins' arms, and taken to the fire station, traffic control tower at the airport and on a canoe ride and so on.

And through that long weekend Louis was so touched by the people and events that surrounded us and all of our activities. It was truly a step back in time for him. And now, here I am again, stepping once more into a part of his past.

Even though he only lived a portion of his life here, it was during the most important and formative years. When he was a young boy growing up, I imagine that Jamestown was very different in some ways but in the important way, the way that it surely is here today, he learned values which I think come first from one's family and then one's friends and neighbors. And these were the values which helped him to get through all those tough lonely years when he was trying so desperately to get started in his writing and it was those values learned as a small child that really made us what we are.

Louis was truly a man of his word and through his example our son and daughter have become young adults who can be depended on. They have gotten me through a great change in my life and I know that thanks to Louis, Beau and Angelique I am able to carry on his work.

School was very important to Louis and the children of school age were always interesting. When he got a letter from a child it was always the first to be answered. Even later in his career when his fan mail became almost overpowering, he certainly always found time for the children. So it is a special thing and a great honor for Louis to have a school named for him.

As I've often said, Louis may have dropped out of school but he never dropped out of education. He was a man of incredible self-discipline and that was truly there, first in his home and later in school. You know we never learn about discipline without first having it imposed upon us by others.

The most important aspect of Louis' education, I think, was his desire and energy for being a better educated and more well rounded human being. His passion for learning never waned through all the years of his life and even the last year he followed his pattern to read at least a hundred books a year, mostly non-fiction. And in <u>Bendigo Shafter</u> he said something about books that has always moved me and I'd like to quote it now. He said,

"Sometimes, I think if it were not for books I could not live, I'd be so lonely. But I can take a book out of that trunk, and it was just like talking to an old friend, and I imagine them as they were, bent over their desks or tables, trying to put what they thought into words."

When things were bad Louis had no money. Many a time he would skip meals so he could buy some books he really wanted. In those days there were no paperback books so a man had to choose what he was going to spend his money on — a movie, a dinner or a book. For Louis it was always a book.

He felt that his own library was his personal time machine and in his room he could talk with important brilliant men and women in history or science or literature or about any subject he chose.

He also felt, and said many times, that the adventure he had in books was the most exciting, far surpassing the days he spent sailing the seas, life in the Chinese army or skinning dead cattle, topping the trees or even working in the mines. He said we needed books, we needed something on which to build a dream, and if he were here today he would most certainly be a strong advocate of the importance of education.

He felt that schools could certainly open up the doors and windows of one's mind and encourage and excite a person to go on further through his life with more and more to be learned. In that search for knowledge everyone's life is truly enriched and made a great endless adventure. And for us, his family, it was and is an extraordinary adventure. In higher education and applied learning his work goes on.

I'd like also to quote from Louis the introduction to a collection of short stories called <u>Yondering</u>. These are stories that came from his own life and I think he can tell a little bit about it much better than I can probably. He said,

"In the beginning there was a dream, a young boy's dream, a dream of far lands to see, of oceans to cross, and somewhere at the trail's end, a girl. The Girl.

"More than all else I wanted to tell stories, stories that people could read and hear, stories to love and remember. I had no desire to write to please those who make it their business to comment, but for the people who do the work of the world, who live on the land or love the land, people who make and bake and struggle to make ends meet, for the people who invent, who design, who build, for the people who do. And if somewhere down the line a man or woman can put a finger on a line and say, 'Yes, that is the way it was. I was there,' then I would be amply repaid.

"I have never scoffed at sentiment. Cynicism is ever the outward face of emptiness.

"What, after all, is romance? It is the music of those who make the world turn, the people who make things happen. Romance is the story of dreams that could come true and so often do.

"Why do men ride the range? Go to sea? Explore the polar ice caps? Why do they ride rockets to unknown worlds? It is because of romance, because of the stories they have read and the stories they have dreamed.

"Some have said this is the age of nonhero, that the day of the hero is gone. That's nonsense. When the hero is gone, man himself will be gone, for the hero is our future, our destiny."

APPENDIX

Alice Remembers

Eleven girls spent a lot of time in the late '30's at beautiful Lake Metigoshe, ten miles north of Bottineau, North Dakota. They grew up in Bottineau where strong ties of friendship developed. This group called themselves the Lakedwellers and are now living miles apart but continue to write and talk with each other.

When planning another reunion in 1986 Margaret Hawkins suggested they meet in Durango, Colorado in hopes they could visit with the L'Amour family who were usually there during the month of August.

They did meet there and were disappointed in only one thing. The L'Amours weren't present because Louis, as a member of the Executive Council of <u>The Center for the Book</u>, was in Washington attending its meeting at the Library of Congress.

Alice Ferguson Kozik, a Lakedweller who lived in California was able to join Margaret for a visit to the L'Amour home. They were taken to dinner and on returning Louis gave a lengthy tour of his study. As this was concluding Kathy gave them a call. Her freshly made rhubarb pie and coffee was ready.

As their visit ended Louis gave Alice an autographed copy of his latest book. The L'Amours waved goodbye from the circular drive. As the two women drove away, neither spoke for a while then Alice said, "Now, there is the most charming man I have ever met."

ABOUT THE AUTHORS

Reese Hawkins is a native of Greer, South Carolina. He received an Associate of Arts from North Greenville Junior College in Tigerville and continued his education at Furman University in Greenville, South Carolina where he received a B.S. degree in Chemistry.

After service in World War II, he earned a B.S. degree in Pharmacy at North Dakota State University in Fargo. For many years Hawkins was pharmacist-owner of drug stores in Gilford College, North Carolina and Jamestown, North Dakota.

After selling his store in 1977 he spent 20 years in his home area in South Carolina. He and his wife, Margaret, moved back to Jamestown in 1998 where he has an office in Meidinger Square. It is here he continues his writing and visits with those who stop by to see their display of L'Amour memorabilia.

Meredith Hawkins Wallin was born in South Carolina and grew up in Jamestown, North Dakota. After receiving degrees from St. Olaf College and St. Cloud State University, she taught art and creative writing in Iowa and Minnesota, then worked as a legal assistant and law firm administrator in New York City. Thereafter she began writing in Pennsylvania and now lives in North Carolina with her daughter and husband, an artist/professor at East Carolina University. In 1997 she received a North Carolina Arts Council grant in literature to pursue her writing.

To order additional copies of
Remembering Louis L'Amour
please complete the following.

$16.95 EACH
*(plus $3.50 shipping & handling for first book,
add $1.00 for each additional book ordered.*

*Shipping and Handling costs for larger quantites
available upon request.*

Please send me _____ additional books at $16.95 + shipping & handling

Bill my: ❏ VISA ❏ MasterCard   Expires _____

Card # _____

Signature _____

Daytime Phone Number _____

For credit card orders call 1-888-568-6329
TO ORDER ON-LINE VISIT: www.jmcompanies.com
OR SEND THIS ORDER FORM TO:
McCleery & Sons Publishing
PO Box 248
Gwinner, ND 58040-0248

I am enclosing $_____   ❏ Check ❏ Money Order
Payable in US funds. No cash accepted.

SHIP TO:

Name_____

Mailing Address _____

City _____

State/Zip _____

Orders by check allow longer delivery time.
Money order and credit card orders will be shipped within 48 hours.
This offer is subject to change without notice.

THE "KAMRON COLLECTION"

Charlie's Gold and Other Frontier Tales
Kamron's first collection of short stories gives you adventure tales about men and women of the west, made up of cowboys, Indians, settlers, gunslingers and other colorful characters. Written by Kent Kamron. (174 pgs.)
$15.95 each in a 6x9" paperback.
(plus $3.50 shipping & handling)

A Time For Justice and Other Frontier Tales
Kamron's second collection of short stories. This book crackles with fourteen more adventure tales of men and women who settled the west. It's chock full of Indians, cavalry and cowboys. Posses chase down bandits and bank robbers, and some downright mean killers lie in wait of judgement day. It's a must for readers of western historical fiction.
Written by Kent Kamron. (196 pgs.)
$16.95 each in a 6x9" paperback.
(plus $3.50 shipping & handling)

The Dime Novel Man and Other Frontier Tales
Kamron's third collection of short stories, due out in 2001. Set in the vein of *Charlie's Gold* and *A Time for Justice,* more memorable characters of dubious nature—both men and women—leave their legacies behind as they tame the land of the western frontier. In paperback, approximately 200 pages.

Dr. Val Farmer's
Honey, I Shrunk The Farm
The first volume in a three part series of Rural Stress Survival Guides discusses the following in seven chapters: Farm Economics; Understanding The Farm Crisis; How To Cope With Hard Times; Families Going Through It Together; Dealing With Debt; Going For Help, Helping Others and Transitions Out of Farming.
Written by Val Farmer. (208 pgs.)
$16.95 each in a 6x9" paperback.

Pay Dirt
An absorbing story reveals how a man with the courage to follow his dream found both gold and unexpected adventure and adversity in Interior Alaska, while learning that human nature can be the most unpredictable of all.
Written by Otis Hahn & Alice Vollmar. (168 pgs.)
$15.95 each in a 6x9" paperback.

It Really Happened Here!
Relive the days of farm-to-farm salesmen and hucksters, of ghost ships and locust plagues when you read Ethelyn Pearson's collection of strange but true tales. It captures the spirit of our ancestors in short, easy to read, colorful accounts that will have you yearning for more.
Written by Ethelyn Pearson. (168 pgs.)
$24.95 each in an 8-1/2x11" paperback.

Country-fied
Stories with a sense of humor and love for country and small town people who, like the author, grew up country-fied . . . Country-fied people grow up with a unique awareness of their dependence on the land. They live their lives with dignity, hard work, determination and the ability to laugh at themselves.
Written by Elaine Babcock. (184 pgs.)
$14.95 each in a 6x9" paperback.
(plus $3.50 in shipping & handling)

Bonanza Belle
In 1908, Carrie Amundson left her home to become employed on a bonanza farm. One tragedy after the other befell her and altered her life considerably, and she found herself back on the farm.
Written by Elaine Ulness Swenson. (344 pgs.)
$15.95 each in a 6x8-1/4" paperback.
(plus $3.50 ea. shipping & handling)

First The Dream
This story spans ninety years of Anna's life. She finds love, loses it, and finds in once again. A secret that Anna has kept is fully revealed at the end of her life.
Written by Elaine Ulness Swenson. (326 pgs.)
$15.95 each in a 6x8-1/4" paperback.
(plus $3.50 ea. shipping & handling)

Pete's New Family
Pete's New Family is a tale for children (ages 4-8) lovingly written to help youngsters understand events of divorce that they are powerless to change. Written by Brenda Jacobson.
$9.95 each in a 5-1/2x8-1/2" paperback.
(plus $2.50 each shipping & handling) (price breaks after qty. of 10)

Prayers For Parker Cookbook
Parker Sebens is a 3 year old boy from Milnor, ND, who lost both of his arms in a tragic farm accident on September 18, 2000. Parker will face many more surgeries in his future, plus be fitted for prothesis.
All profits from the sale of this book will go to the Parker Sebens' Benefit Fund, a fund set up to help with medical-related expenses due to Parker's accident. $8.00 ea. in a 5-1/4"x8-1'4" spiral bound book.
(plus $2.00 ea. shipping & handling)